TAKE TEN...
Steps to
Successful Research

TAKE TEN...
Steps to
Successful Research

LIZ ROTHLEIN, Ed.D.
ANITA MEYER MEINBACH, Ed.D.

Scott, Foresman and Company
GLENVIEW, ILLINOIS   LONDON

Good Year Books

are available for preschool through grade 12 and for every basic curriculum subject plus many enrichment areas. For more Good Year Books, contact your local bookseller or educational dealer. For a complete catalog with information about other Good Year Books, please write:

Good Year Books
Department GYB
1900 East Lake Avenue
Glenview, Illinois 60025

ISBN 0-673-38087-4

Portions of pp. 74–77 from *Unlocking the Secrets of Research* by Anita Meyer Meinbach and Liz Christman Rothlein, Copyright © 1986 Scott, Foresman and Company.

To Ash, my inspiration.

L.R.

To my parents, Lucille and Alan Meyer, who made me believe
that anything is possible.

A.M.M.

Acknowledgments

We offer our gratitude and appreciation to the individuals who have been instrumental in the preparation of this book: Christopher Jennison, who believed in this project and whose encouragement, advice, and guidance helped us each step of the way; Dr. Carole Bernstein, whose input and generosity we depended upon; and Karen Herzog, who offered thoughtful feedback and support. We also thank Nancy Whitelaw, who reviewed the manuscript and offered helpful suggestions.

CONTENTS

Introduction / ix
Rationale / ix
Objectives / ix
Features / ix

Take Ten: Student Checklist / xi

Take Ten: Teacher Checklist / xiii

Teacher-Directed Activities / xv

Alternatives to the Research Paper / xix

Step 1:
Choosing the Subject / 1

Step 2:
Narrowing/Focusing the Subject / 7

Step 3:
Selecting Appropriate Reference Materials / 13

Step 4:
Formulating a Thesis Statement / 21

Step 5:
Writing the Outline / 29

Step 6:
Preparing Note Cards and Taking Notes / 37

Step 7:
Revising the Outline / 47

Step 8:
Writing the First Draft / 55

Step 9:
Revising the First Draft / 65

Step 10:
Writing the Final Copy / 73

Answer Section / 79

INTRODUCTION

Rationale

Research can be a stimulating challenge, an exploration in which the synthesis of information can reinforce or alter ideas, encourage opinions, inspire change, and provoke thought. Unfortunately, students often perceive the research process to be overwhelming. They approach the task haphazardly, giving little thought to the analysis and evaluation of the information provided.

To become successful researchers, students must approach research in a logical, sequential manner. Taking students from the selection of a topic for research to the final revision, *Take Ten . . . Steps to Successful Research* provides a simple and effective procedure for doing research. For each of the ten steps of research described in this book, activities are provided to facilitate ease in the research process.

It is especially hoped that *Take Ten . . . Steps to Successful Research* will help students develop life-long thinking skills, work habits, and commitments to knowledge and understanding.

Objectives

This book is designed to enable students to develop several vital thinking and learning objectives. Through completion of the activities included, the student will:

- become more proficient at each step of the research process.
- develop skills in the analysis and evaluation of information.
- develop skills in the synthesis of information.
- become familiar with a variety of reference sources.
- become aware of the importance of research in all aspects of work.
- develop skills in using and writing footnotes and bibliographies.
- develop independent work skills and strategies.

Features

Take Ten . . . Steps to Successful Research is a comprehensive book that describes each step of the research process in a sequential and easy-to-follow manner. Students in grades 5 and up will benefit from the materials presented as they gain insight into the research process and develop research skills, as well as confidence in doing research.

The book consists of the following features:

Take Ten: Checklists

The student checklist provides a systematic way for students to document their progress as they move through the ten steps in the research process.

The teacher checklist provides a means for monitoring students' progress. As students complete skills at each step, the teacher can evaluate and record their work.

Teacher-Directed Activities

Teacher-directed activities are provided for each step of the research process. These supplementary activities enable the teacher to further improve the research skills introduced and developed through the activity sheets.

Alternatives to the Research Paper

The organization and formats for debates, speeches, problem solving, and courtroom dramas are included as alternatives to the written research paper. These ideas and activities, while encouraging students to use the research process, result in a variety of types of final products.

Activity Sheets

The activity sheets for each of the ten steps are divided into three sections: "Getting Started," "Activities," and "On Your Own." "Getting Started" introduces students to each step of the research process. Pertinent information is provided to the student to facilitate understanding of the step. The numbered "Activities" develop skills to foster proficiency at each step of the research process. Many of the skills are first introduced in a basic manner, and subsequent activities develop the skills more fully. While providing practice for the designated steps, the "Activities" are also designed to develop the higher-order thinking skills, as students analyze, synthesize, and evaluate information uncovered through participation in the research process. "On Your Own" activity sheets afford students the opportunity to transfer knowledge and apply their research skills by involving them in the planning, organization, and development of their own independent research project.

Editing Checklist

The Editing Checklist included with Step 9 provides a systematic way for students to check the contents and oganization of their research paper prior to writing the final draft. The checklist helps students to individually proofread and edit their research paper and encourages feedback from an editing partner.

Writing a Bibliography

The procedure, format, and examples for writing a bibliography are provided with Step 10 to enable students to compile a bibliography.

Writing Footnotes

The procedure, format, and examples for writing footnotes are provided with Step 10 to enable students to correctly cite their reference sources.

Reference Sources

An annotated list of sources is provided in Step 3 to acquaint students with the variety of reference materials available and to encourage them to seek out and use these sources.

Answer Key

The answer key facilitates teacher evaluation of the activity sheets.

TAKE TEN
Student Checklist

NAME

DONE ✓

STEP 1	**Choose a Subject**	◯
STEP 2	**Narrow/Focus the Subject**	◯
STEP 3	**Select Appropriate Reference Materials**	◯
STEP 4	**Formulate a Thesis Statement**	◯
STEP 5	**Write an Outline**	◯
STEP 6	**Prepare Note Cards and Take Notes**	◯
STEP 7	**Revise the Outline**	◯
STEP 8	**Write the First Draft**	◯
STEP 9	**Revise the First Draft**	◯
STEP 10	**Write the Final Copy**	◯

TAKE TEN

Teacher Checklist

NAMES

Step	Title	Activities	Status markers
STEP 1	Choosing the subject	ACTIVITIES 1 2 3 4	O Y O
STEP 2	Narrowing/focusing the subject	ACTIVITIES 1 2 3 4	O Y O
STEP 3	Selecting appropriate reference materials	ACTIVITIES 1 2 3 4 5	O Y O
STEP 4	Formulating a thesis statement	ACTIVITIES 1 2 3 4 5	O Y O
STEP 5	Writing the outline	ACTIVITIES 1 2 3 4	O Y O
STEP 6	Reporting note cards and taking notes	ACTIVITIES 1 2 3 4 5	O Y O

TAKE TEN **Teacher Checklist**		STEP 7 Revising the outline ACTIVITIES			STEP 8 Writing the first draft ACTIVITIES					STEP 9 Revising the first draft ACTIVITIES					STEP 10 Writing the final copy ACTIVITIES			Additional Comments
NAMES		1	2	3	1	2	3	4		1	2	3	4		1	2		

TEACHER-DIRECTED ACTIVITIES

Introducing the Book

1. Discuss the subjects of "research" and "reference materials" with students. The following questions may help with this discussion:

- When you hear the word "research," what ideas come to mind?
- What is meant by the term "research"?
- Why is it important to know how to research a particular subject?
- How are researchers like detectives?
- What tools does a detective use? What tools will a researcher use?
- If you could learn more about any subject, what would you choose?

2. Explain the format of the activities. Each step is divided into three main sections: "Getting Started," which introduces students to the step of the research process; "Activities," which develops skills in the step; and "On Your Own," which helps students pursue their own research subject.

Step 1: Choosing the Subject

1. Ask students to compile a journal or daily log of ideas and subjects that interest them. These ideas/subjects may be ones they read about, hear about on television, or learn about in class or simply ideas that just occur to them as they daydream. Allow a certain amount of time daily or weekly in which the students can pursue these subjects without the pressure of a specific assignment or grade. When it is time for them to choose a subject for their own independent research (Step 1), students may wish to select a subject from the list in their journals.

2. Provide students with an "interest inventory." After they have completed this inventory, ask them whether their responses have generated any subjects for further research. Students may wish to select one of these subjects when it is time for them to do their own independent research.

3. Have students survey the subjects in their various textbooks and list those subjects in which they are most interested. They may wish to choose a subject from this list when it is time for them to choose a subject for their own independent research.

Step 2: Narrowing/Focusing the Subject

1. Involve students in a game similar to ghost. The first student begins by suggesting a broad subject. Each subsequent student narrows the subject further until the subject becomes too narrow for effective research. A student may "challenge" a topic that he or she feels has been narrowed too far, and the student who offered this subject must then defend his or her subject. The class can vote to decide the question.

2. Give each student a copy of a newspaper or magazine article in which you feel he or she would be particularly interested. Ask the students to read their articles and then determine subjects they might pursue if they were to do additional research. List these subjects on the chalkboard or a chart and discuss each as to whether it is properly narrowed/focused.

3. Involve the students in a class brainstorming session. Allow students to suggest several favorite subjects and brainstorm ways in which each subject can be narrowed/focused in order to develop good, manageable subjects for research.

Step 3: Selecting Appropriate Reference Materials

1. Give a brief overview of each reference source listed in "Getting Started," Step 3. Read some especially interesting information from each source in order to motivate students to use these materials.

2. Divide students into groups. Assign a specific reference source to each group. Have the groups create a skit to advertise this reference source.

3. Using the focused subject that students have selected for individual research (Step 2), direct students to locate information on that subject from sources other than the library. For example, provide students with a list of government agencies to which they might write for free or inexpensive materials related to their subject. When appropriate, encourage students to develop a questionnaire that could be used to interview specific people or that could be mailed to appropriate sources to obtain additional information.

4. You may want to use *Unlocking the Secrets of Research* by Meinbach and Rothlein (Scott, Foresman, 1986) to introduce students to a wide variety of reference materials and to help them develop skills in selecting appropriate reference materials.

Step 4: Formulating a Thesis Statement

1. Choose a variety of research papers to share with students. Give them the opportunity to identify the thesis statement in each one. Also, discuss the ways in which each author achieved his or her purpose.

2. Divide students into groups of four. Allow each group to select a subject for research. Have them brainstorm the ideas/questions that should be included in this research. Based on one idea or a combination of ideas, have the group prepare a thesis statement. Allow time for the groups to share their thesis statements.

Step 5: Writing the Outline

1. Give a lecture on a topic most students find interesting. Have students outline the lecture, dividing information received into main topics, subtopics, and details. Put a few of the outlines on the chalkboard and discuss how well they include all the points from the lecture. Discuss ways in which each outline can be improved. Repeat this process at various times throughout the year.

2. Set up a concrete outline using actual objects. For example, for the subject Items in the Classroom, the following outline can be created (arrange the actual items rather than having students simply write them):

I. Classroom equipment
  A. Desks
  B. Chairs
  C. Charts
II. Students' tools
  A. Pens
    1. Black
    2. Blue
    3. Red
  B. Pencils
    1. Regular
    2. Colored
  C. Crayons
  D. Paper
    1. Lined
    2. Unlined

Step 6: Preparing Note Cards and Taking Notes

1. Have students take notes on a specific lecture, film, or brief article. Give a quiz based on the material and allow students to use their notes when taking the quiz. After going over the answers, discuss how complete their notes were and how the notes could be improved. What problems did they have? How can these problems be avoided in the future?

2. Distribute a copy of the same article to all students. Have them take notes on the article. When they have completed their note taking, have students evaluate their notes as they answer the following questions:

- What was the main idea of the article? Did I include this in my notes?
- What important facts did the article discuss? Did I include these facts in my notes?
- What important statistics or quotations did the article state to support the main idea? Did I include them in my notes?

3. Distribute a copy of an article from a book, magazine, or newspaper. (Students may be given the same article or different articles.) Explain to students that the information in the article is of extreme importance and must be forwarded by telegraph across the continent. They must then express the main idea and any important supporting details in a telegram of 25 words or less.

Step 7: Revising the Outline

1. Give students an outline in which the organization of main topics, subtopics, and details is haphazard. Have students revise the outline to reflect the organization they would use if this outline were the basis of a research paper.

2. Select a subject for research that would be of interest to the students. Brainstorm ideas that would be included in a research paper and, as a class, create an outline for the subject. Provide two or three related articles. Have students revise the outline depending on the information found in the articles. Students should pretend that this is the only information available on the subject; as a result, they will need to add or delete main topics, subtopics, and details.

Step 8: Writing the First Draft

1. Provide the class with an outline on a subject of interest. Brainstorm possible thesis statements for a research paper based on the outline. Allow students to divide into small groups, each group selecting a different thesis. Depending on the thesis selected, have each group write an introduction and a conclusion for the subject outlined. Remind them of the importance of writing an interesting introduction that will grab and hold the reader's attention, as well as an effective conclusion. Allow time for the groups to share and critique the introductions and conclusions.

2. Divide the class into small groups. Have each group write a 25-word telegram on a selected topic. The telegram will then serve as the only information the others have on that specific topic. Each of the other groups is to expand on the telegram, just as they would expand on notes when writing their first draft. Compare the different ways in which the groups have written their paragraphs based on the telegram.

3. Provide the class with an outline about a familiar object, such as a pen, a bicycle, or a model train. Divide students into groups and have each group write an introduction and a conclusion based not only on the outline but on one of the following purposes:

•Relate the object to its importance in the world.
•Compare the object with a quality in children.
•Defend the object's style and design.
•Describe how different life would be without this object.

Allow time for the groups to share their introductions and conclusions.

Step 9: Revising the First Draft

1. Have students select a favorite comic strip. Using a thesaurus, see how many different words they can find for the original words (nouns, verbs, adjectives, adverbs) written in the comic strip. Have them rewrite the comic strip using words they have found.

2. Go over the various errors that can be made in writing. Also, review the editing symbols with students. Demonstrate these symbols by writing several incorrect sentences on the board and allowing students to make the corrections.

3. Following creative writing exercises, allow students to practice their editing skills. Have them select editing partners and analyze their work:

- Is the introduction interesting and exciting? How can it be improved?
- Are there any spelling or punctuation errors?
- Could other words be substituted for less-effective words?
- Is the main point clear? If not, how can the paper be changed to make it clear?
- Are the sentences and paragraphs in the correct order?
- Is the ending appropriate? If not, how can it be changed?

OPTIONAL: Have the editing partners circle the *best* sentence in the papers. Have students rewrite their papers building on these sentences.

Step 10: Writing the Final Copy

1. Discuss with students the criteria that should be used to evaluate research papers. Criteria might include:

- Significance or importance of the work.
- How well it addresses the audience for which it is intended.
- How well it synthesizes information from a variety of sources.
- How effective it is in accomplishing the purpose (thesis) for which it was written.
- Insights gained from the paper.

2. Have students evaluate research papers, including their own, based on the criteria.

3. Allow time for students to share their research and answer any questions based on their findings.

ALTERNATIVES TO THE RESEARCH PAPER

Research is usually thought of in terms of the "research paper." Both teachers and students generally consider the research paper to be the end product, while all the steps in between are simply a means to that end. Research, however, should be an integral part of the learning experience. The skills developed through research afford students the opportunity to develop the capacity to integrate knowledge, analyze and synthesize information, and reach their own conclusions.

Many strategies can be employed in the classroom that encourage research, yet result in end products quite different from the traditional research paper. In addition to developing research skills, such activities as debate, problem solving, speech writing, and courtroom drama foster critical and creative thinking skills and promote independent learning. This section is provided to help you implement such strategies. The information should also serve as a springboard for other activities that will similarly involve students in exciting, stimulating, and challenging research-related experiences.

Debate

Debate is an argument presented by two teams, each arguing a different side of the issue. Debate necessitates preparation, and much of this preparation requires research—collecting and organizing ideas, and evaluating the information found. In debate, the argument is only as good as the information and evidence found to support the proposition. The contest is won by the team that presents the best argument.

Organization of the Debate

The most frequently used form of debate in high school is the cross examination. However, depending on the level and maturity of your group, this form will have to be modified. The order of speakers and the time alloted for the cross examination form of debate is as follows:

First affirmative	8 minutes
Negative cross examination	3 minutes
First negative	8 minutes
Affirmative cross examination	3 minutes
Second affirmative	8 minutes
Negative cross examination	3 minutes
Second negative	8 minutes
Affirmative cross examination	3 minutes
First negative rebuttal	4 minutes
First affirmative rebuttal	4 minutes
Second negative rebuttal	4 minutes
Second affirmative rebuttal	4 minutes

The affirmative team must start the debate by explaining a problem and a need for change. The first and second affirmative speeches should be carefully planned, outlined, and rehearsed.

The negative team has to prove that the affirmative team's case should not be accepted. Both the first and second negative speeches should be carefully planned, outlined, and rehearsed.

In the second affirmative speech, as well as in both negative speeches, debaters need to "refute" the arguments made by the opposing team. To refute an argument is to break it down by recognizing faulty statements, illogical reasoning, and so on.

In the cross examination, the debaters are allowed to ask questions of an opponent. The cross examination is used to clarify a point made by the opponent, to expose errors in the opponent's argument, or to try to get the opponent to admit something damaging.

The rebuttal is used to help each side rebuild its case after the cross examination by the opposing team. New arguments cannot be introduced in the rebuttal, but new evidence is allowed. The first negative and second affirmative rebuttals should restate the issues involved in the debate.

Topics for Debate

Selecting the topic for debate should take into account the interests of students, their maturity in dealing with certain subject matters, and the significance of the topic itself. Current events usually provide a wealth of ideas for debate, and the selection of a topic should be timely. Issues for debate could include book banning, the limiting of nuclear weapons, funding for space exploration, euthanasia, capital punishment, welfare laws, or increasing the number of hours in a school day.

Problem Solving

In problem solving, students first identify a problem, then follow several steps to determine the best solution, and , finally, plan its implementation. Research is an important step in the problem-solving process, since students must be aware of all aspects of the problem. Research provides information, perceptions, and other important data. "Creative problem solving" and "future problem solving" strategies are gaining widespread acceptance in the classroom and are the basis of many nationwide competitions. The problem-solving procedure, however, should not be limited to competitions and should be used by students whenever they encounter a problem.

Steps to Problem Solving

1. Fact finding. Students should analyze a problem situation and brainstorm as many related problems as possible. Students must research the situation at this step in order to gather the information necessary to understand all aspects and implications of the situation.

2. Problem finding. Have students identify the *underlying problem* or problem that they feel is most important. Tell them to think of the situation in terms of "In what ways might we . . ." or "How might I . . ." do a specific thing in order to help alleviate or improve the situation. Students must sort through the information researched to identify that which is most relevant.

3. Idea finding. Have students brainstorm as many possible solutions to the underlying problem as possible.

4. Solution finding. Have students identify the criteria most important for judging the solutions For example, if the problem identified is "How might we establish a program for involving the elderly in school projects?" one

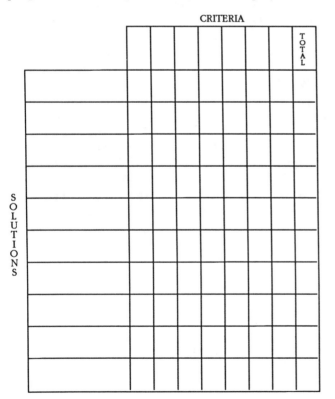

of the criteria for judging the solutions might be based on cost. Help students use these criteria to evaluate the best solutions from Step 3. They can use the accompanying grid to rank the solutions. For example, suppose you are evaluating ten solutions. Based on criterion 1, rank the solution that is best with a 10, the next best with a 9, and so on until all the solutions have been ranked for that criteria. This procedure can be followed for each of the criteria listed. The final step is to add the points for each solution to find the solution that best meets all established criteria.

5. Have students describe the best solution, explain how it will be implemented, and list what needs to be done.

Because this is only a brief explanation of the steps in problem solving, you may wish to consult one of the following sources for additional information and guidelines:

Feldhusen, J. F., and Treffinger, D. J. *Teaching Creative Thinking and Problem Solving.* Dubuque, Iowa: Kendall/Hunt Publishing Co., 1977.

Eberle, B., and Stanish, B. *CPS for Kids: A Resource Book for Teaching Creative Problem Solving to Children.* Buffalo, N.Y.: D.O.K., 1980.

Noller, R. B., Parnes, S. J., and Biondi, A. M. *Creative Actionbook: Revised Edition of Creative Behavior Workbook.* New York: Charles Scribner's Sons, 1976.

Topics for Problem Solving
Topics for problem solving can range from problems perceived in the environment to situations in the individual's life or problems experienced by the entire class. Examples include the plight of farmers in America, terrorism, funding for education, and improving grades in school. Provide students with a brief explanation of situations from which students can then identify problems and continue through the steps outlined.

Speech Writing
Expressing themselves in front of a group is often extremely difficult for students. It is important, therefore, to involve students in preparing and delivering speeches. As with most things, the more practice they have in this area, the easier it will become. As students plan speeches, they will naturally be involved in the research process. Most of the steps in writing a research paper can be used to facilitate the planning, organization and writing of a speech. In addition, as students gain experience in oral communication, they will develop confidence and poise.

Format of Speeches

Writing an outline, taking notes using appropriate sources, and revising the outline will help students in the preparation of their speech. Most speeches include the following parts:

1. Introduction. Similar to the introduction for a research paper, a speech's introduction should capture the audience's attention.

2. Thesis statement. This statement makes the audience aware of the purpose for the speech—the point the speaker wants to make.

3. Development. Facts, quotations, anecdotes, comparisons, statistics, and so on are used to develop the points the speaker wishes to make. Often, visual aids can help make the speech more interesting and understandable.

4. Conclusion. At the end of the speech the speaker reviews the main points and gives the audience something to think about.

No matter how excellent the speech may be, it will not be effective unless the delivery is good. Practicing the speech will help students with their delivery. They should also be reminded to use good posture, to speak in a well-modulated voice, and to look at their audience. Students should learn their speech well enough that they need only glance down at brief notes they've written on note cards. As students rehearse their speeches, suggest that they tape themselves giving the speech, using either audio or video equipment. Have them evaluate the speech and its delivery in order to make it even better.

Topics for Speeches

As students plan their speeches, they must keep in mind their purpose, their audience, and the time frame in which they have to speak. There are three main purposes for speeches: to inform, to persuade, or to entertain. It is important to involve students in writing for each of the purposes. Informative speeches present information. For example, an informational speech might tell about the life of a famous person, describe a special event, or explain the procedure for baking a cake. Persuasive speeches are designed to convince the audience to think or act in a certain way. Persuasive speeches can encourage the audience to vote for a certain candidate, to change toothpaste brands, or to alter television viewing habits. Entertaining speeches are designed to bring enjoyment to the audience. They can be humorous or serious. They can also be persuasive and informational as well as entertaining.

Courtroom Drama

Involving students in courtroom trials is another excellent strategy for enhancing research skills as well as improving oral communication skills. Through researching a specific case, the various testimonies involved, and applicable laws, students will further develop their critical thinking skills as they analyze, synthesize, and draw conclusions.

Participants and Their Roles

Judge: Acts as referee for the opposing sides: the prosecution and the defense. The judge is the authority on the law and, based on the evidence presented, determines whether the accused is guilty or innocent. If the accused is found guilty, the judge is responsible for determining the penalty for the crime. If a jury is present, the judge does not decide on guilt or innocence but does decide on the sentence.

As judge, the student is responsible for researching the laws pertaining to the case and must give instructions to the jury (if one is present) regarding the laws that apply. The judge must also be prepared to rule on what evidence may be submitted during the trial.

Jury: Tries the facts, weighs the evidence presented by both sides, and determines the guilt or innocence of the accused.

As part of the jury, students should listen carefully to all testimony and determine what is fact and what is opinion.

Witnesses: Present information based on prior knowledge.

Witnesses should meet with either the defense attorney or prosecuting attorney and be familiar with the role to be played.

Prosecutor: In a criminal trial, must decide whether to bring a case to trial and must present the evidence against the defendant (the person being accused). In a civil case, represents the plaintiff (the injured party) in court and prepares the case against the defendant.

As prosecutor, the student must list all facts from the case that show the defendant is guilty. The prosecuting attorney should list reasons why the plaintiff has a right to bring the accused to trial. The prosecutor should be familiar with laws pertaining to the case and prepare the opening remarks and closing argument.

Plaintiff: Brings charges against another person.

The plaintiff must advise the prosecuting attorney and assist him or her in preparation of the case.

Defendant: Is the accused.

The defendant must advise the defense attorney and assist him or her in the preparation of the case.

Defense attorney: Attempts to persuade the jury or the judge that the defendant is innocent of the charges.

As defense attorney, the student should list all facts from the case that show the defendant is not guilty of a crime. He or she needs to be familiar with laws pertaining to the case and should prepare the opening remarks and closing argument.

Bailiff: Sees that order is maintained in the court.

Court reporter: Records the trial.

Types of Cases

A trial can be either criminal or civil. You may wish to base cases on real situations or trials that have existed, or devise those of your own. Cases based on fictional characters are quite popular with students. For example, you may wish to charge Hansel and Gretel with trespassing, or charge the parents of Hansel and Gretel with child abuse.

Choosing the Subject

S T E P 1

You've been asked to write a research paper, but where do you begin? First of all, don't let the word "research" scare you! Research can be exciting and challenging. In order for research to be a rewarding experience, you must be familiar with the ten steps to research. Once you are comfortable with these steps, you will discover that research really can be fun!

The first step, and one of the most important tasks you will have to do, is to choose a subject for your research. The following ideas can help you with your selection:

1. The subject you choose should be interesting to you.

2. You do not have to know much about the subject in order to select it. You only need a desire to want to learn more about it.

3. Make sure the subject is worthy of the time you will be spending to research it.

ACTIVITY ONE   *CHOOSING A SUBJECT*

I. DIRECTIONS: For each of the following broad areas of interest, select a subject that you would be interested in researching.

Sports   _____

Strange phenomena   _____

Monsters   _____

Traditions   _____

Astronauts   _____

Politicians   _____

Careers   _____

Underwater exploration   _____

II. DIRECTIONS: Now that you have chosen the subject you find most interesting within each area, select *one* and explain why you chose the subject you did. What about it did you find interesting?

Area _____   **Subject** _____

Explanation _____

1

ACTIVITY TWO _CHOOSING A SUBJECT_

Directions: Select a variety of national magazines, such as _Time, Newsweek,_ or _Sports Illustrated,_ that contain factual information. Skim through these magazines and locate three articles that you find especially interesting. For each of these articles, fill in the blanks below.

Article title: _____ **Source:** _____

Summary: _____

_____

_____

_____

If you were to do further reading based on this article, what subject would you research?

_____

Article title: _____ **Source:** _____

Summary: _____

_____

_____

_____

If you were to do further reading based on this article, what subject would you research?

_____

Article title: _____ **Source:** _____

Summary: _____

_____

_____

_____

If you were to do further reading based on this article, what subject would you research?

_____

S T E P

1

CHOOSING A SUBJECT ACTIVITY THREE

I. DIRECTIONS: From each of the broad areas in the boxes listed below, think of (brainstorm) as many related subjects as you can. Let your mind go and be as creative as possible. List these subjects in the appropriate boxes. (Complete the brainstorming for one area before moving on to the next.)

OLYMPIC GAMES	MAGIC

TELEVISION	GREAT AMERICANS

II. DIRECTIONS: Look at the subjects you have listed in each box. Draw a line through any of the subjects that you do not find interesting or that you do not feel are worthy of spending time to research. From the subjects remaining in each box, draw a circle around the one that you would most like to research.

ACTIVITY FOUR   *CHOOSING A SUBJECT*

Directions:
Obtain a copy of your local newspaper. Read the headlines concerning national news. From these headlines, choose the three that are the most interesting to you. List these headlines in the appropriate spaces below. Next, read the articles that accompany the headlines. List the subjects that you would research if you wanted to learn more about the topics discussed in the articles. Be sure to choose subjects that are interesting to you and that are worthy of additional research.

Headline # 1 _____

Name of newspaper _____ **Date:** _____

Related subjects   1. _____

                          2. _____

                          3 _____

                          4. _____

Headline # 2 _____

Name of newspaper _____ **Date:** _____

Related subjects   1. _____

                          2. _____

                          3 _____

                          4. _____

Headline # 3 _____

Name of newspaper _____ **Date:** _____

Related subjects   1. _____

                          2. _____

                          3 _____

                          4. _____

ON YOUR OWN

Choosing the Subject

S T E P 1

It's time for you to choose a subject for your own independent research! Remember, when selecting a subject, it is important that you choose one that you find especially interesting and would like to learn about, as well as one that is worthy of the time you will be spending to research it.

1. Skim through various newspapers and magazines to find articles that capture your interest. On the lines below, list subjects related to the articles.

_____   _____
_____   _____
_____   _____
_____   _____
_____   _____
_____   _____
_____   _____

2. Look over the subjects you have listed and decide which of them you'd like to choose as the basis of your independent research. List your subject choice in the box below, as well as the date and your signature.

The Subject of My Research Will Be:

_____

_____

_____

_____   _____
Signature   Date

REMINDER: Check off "Step 1: Choose a Topic" on your Student Checklist.

Narrowing/Focusing the Subject

STEP 2

Now that you have chosen your subject, the next step is to narrow or focus this subject. Keep the following ideas in mind when narrowing/focusing the subject:

1. Narrow/focus your subject so that it is not too general. You will want to select a subject that you feel you can research completely and comprehensively.

2. Make sure that your subject is not too narrow. You will want to select a subject about which you will be able to find enough information.

3. As you focus/narrow your subject, make sure you have chosen some aspect of the subject that especially interests you.

ACTIVITY ONE *NARROWING/FOCUSING THE SUBJECT*

Directions: Listed below are groups of related subjects. For each group decide which topics are too general and which would be the best focused for research. Put a check next to the subject that is the best focused. For example, which of the following would be the best focused subject?

Mars	**Astronomy**	**The Canals of Mars**

You would put a check next to "The Canals of Mars." "Astronomy" would be too general. Volumes have been written on this subject, and it would be difficult to write a comprehensive paper unless you had years to research it. If you were to focus this topic, you might select the subject "Mars." However, even this subject would be too general and needs to be narrowed further, since there are so many aspects of the planet that could be investigated. Thus, "The Canals of Mars" would be the best-focused subject in this group.

1. ☐ California Gold Rush
☐ Panning for Gold
☐ Gold

2. ☐ Navajo Indians
☐ Life on the Reservation
☐ Totem Poles

3. ☐ Types of Cancer
☐ Radiation Therapy
☐ Causes of Cancer

4. ☐ Nutrients in Milk
☐ Dairy Farms
☐ History of the Milk Industry

STEP 2

ACTIVITY TWO *NARROWING/FOCUSING THE SUBJECT*

Directions: For each of the topics listed below, write the word "general" or "narrow" to describe whether the topic is too general or too narrow. On the line below each topic explain why it is either too general or too narrow and suggest a related topic that would be more suitable for research. The first one is done for you.

1. Canals *general*
There are many different canals (Panama, Suez, etc.). There are many aspects to canals, such as purposes and building of canal locks.
Related focused subject *Purposes of canal locks.*

2. World War II _____

_____

_____

Related focused subject _____

3. Location and Size of the Canary Islands _____

_____

_____

Related focused subject _____

4. U.F.O.'s (Unidentified Flying Objects) _____

_____

_____

Related focused subject _____

5. Mickey Mantle's Batting Record _____

_____

_____

Related focused subject _____

NARROWING/FOCUSING THE SUBJECT   ACTIVITY THREE

I. DIRECTIONS: In the spaces following each of the subjects listed below, continue narrowing each subject until you arrive at a subject that you feel is suitable for research. You may not need to use all the spaces provided. The first one is done for you.

1. Law
1. *Development of Law*
2. *Early Influences*
3. *Influences of the Greeks on Law*
4. _____

2. Europe
1. _____
2. _____
3. _____
4. _____

3. Motion Pictures
1. _____
2. _____
3. _____
4. _____

4. Dreams
1. _____
2. _____
3. _____
4. _____

5. Famous Musicians
1. _____
2. _____
3. _____
4. _____

II. DIRECTIONS: Look up the following topics in the encyclopedia. Select subheadings that you feel would be good topics for a research paper. Write these topics on the lines provided.

1. Space
1. _____
2. _____
3. _____
4. _____

2. Atom Bomb
1. _____
2. _____
3. _____
4. _____

3. Indians
1. _____
2. _____
3. _____
4. _____

4. Dinosaurs
1. _____
2. _____
3. _____
4. _____

ACTIVITY FOUR *NARROWING/FOCUSING THE SUBJECT*

Directions: Narrow/focus the subjects in the boxes below through a process called "semantic mapping." To create a semantic map, think of all the words you can that are related to the word in the center of each box. Don't judge any of your responses, and allow your mind to make associations. This mapping process not only allows you to narrow your subject but also helps you to think of topics you might not have otherwise considered.

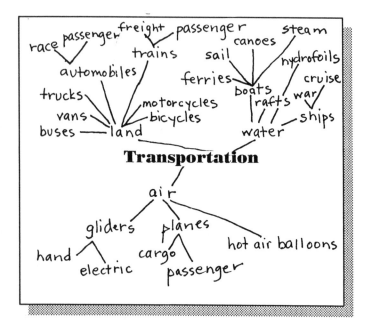

Transportation

Mythology

Drugs

The Elderly

From *Take Ten . . . Steps to Successful Research*, Copyright © 1988 Scott, Foresman and Company.

ON YOUR OWN

Narrowing/Focusing the Subject

It's time for you to narrow the subject you chose to research. Remember, when narrowing/focusing the subject, you want to select a topic that is not too general or too narrow. Be sure to select a topic you are interested in learning more about.

1. On the line below, fill in the subject you selected for research at the end of Step 1.

_____

2. Read a general article concerning this subject. You may wish to consult an encyclopedia, newspaper, or national periodical. This will give you a general understanding of the subject and aid in focusing it.

3. Look at the way the article you have read is organized. If subheadings are provided in the article, list them on the lines below. If subheadings are not provided, create your own by narrowing the subject, and list these topics on the lines below.

_____   _____

_____   _____

_____   _____

4. In the center of the box below, place the subject you selected in Step 1 and create a semantic map for this subject.

Continued next page

5. Look over both the subheadings you listed in #3 above and the words generated in the semantic map. From the topics listed, select a narrowed/focused subject for your independent research. List your new subject choice in the box below, and provide the date and your signature.

The Subject of My Focused Research Will Be:

_____

_____

_____

_____   _____
Signature   Date

REMINDER: Check off "Step 2: Narrow/Focus the Topic" on your Student Checklist.

Selecting Appropriate Reference Materials

Now that you have learned to narrow your subject, the next step is to locate information concerning that subject. Because there are so many reference materials from which to choose, it is important that you select the sources that provide the *most relevant* information for your subject. When selecting appropriate reference materials, consider the following ideas:

1. Make sure that there are sufficient reference materials available that contain information on your subject. If you cannot locate enough information on your subject, you will want to consider an alternate one.

2. The library is probably the best source of information. However, you may wish to gather information from such other sources such as interviews, pamphlets, questionnaires, and so on. You will need to begin to collect information from these sources well in advance.

3. There are three main sources of information in the library: the card catalog, encyclopedias, and the *Readers' Guide to Periodical Literature*. These and other important reference materials are described below. It is essential that you use a variety of materials when involved in research; *do not* rely on any one source. The sources listed are some of the most commonly used reference materials. There are, however, many other sources, in all fields of study, that provide current and useful information.

General Works

Card Catalog. This alphabetized group of cards lists all the books found in the library. Books are listed in the card catalog in three ways: by author, by title, and by subject. Cards provide a brief summary of the book and bibliographical information.

Dictionaries. There are many types of dictionaries. They contain the words used in our language: their meanings, correct pronunciations, syllabication, accents, parts of speech, origin, and so on. Dictionaries also include information such as abbreviations, origins of words, units of measure, and identification of people and places.

Encyclopedias. These comprehensive reference works contain information on a wide range of subjects or on numerous aspects of a particular field.

Familiar Quotations. Quotation references collect famous passages, phrases, and proverbs.

First Facts. These books provide a record of first happenings, discoveries, and inventions.

Thesaurus. A thesaurus contains numerous synonyms for words; it usually gives antonyms as well.

World Almanacs. An almanac provides all types of statistical information, including a yearly calendar of days, weeks, and months, with astronomical data and weather forecasts.

Atlases. An atlas provides geographical and statistical information in the form of maps and pictures.

Specific Works

Current Biography Yearbook. This reference book provides brief information about living leaders in all fields.

Readers' Guide to Periodical Literature. This multivolume reference lists, by subject, the various magazine articles that deal with that subject. Articles can be located by author name as well. Included are the magazine name, volume, date of publication, and page on which the information can be found.

Twentieth Century Authors. This book contains information on the lives of writers of this century from all nations of the world whose works appear in English.

Webster's Biographical Dictionary. This reference work provides biographies of famous people of all nationalities, living and dead.

Who's Who in America. This series of books contains brief information about famous Americans who were living at the time of publication.

 *SELECTING APPROPRIATE*
REFERENCE MATERIALS

Directions: To select the best reference materials for your research, you must be familiar with the materials available in your school (or local) library. Using the list below, locate those reference works that are available. As you find each of the materials, place a check to the left of the appropriate item. On the line following each resource, indicate its location in the library.

❑ Card catalog _____

❑ Dictionary _____

❑ Encyclopedia _____

❑ Familiar quotations _____

❑ First facts _____

❑ Thesaurus _____

❑ World almanac _____

❑ World atlas _____

❑ *Current Biography Yearbook* _____

❑ *Readers' Guide to Periodical Literature* _____

❑ *Twentieth Century Authors* _____

❑ *Webster's Biographical Dictionary* _____

❑ *Who's Who in America* _____

❑ Newspapers _____

❑ Magazines _____

❑ Microfilm _____

❑ Filmstrips _____

❑ Cassette tapes/records _____

❑ Photograph file _____

SELECTING APPROPRIATE REFERENCE MATERIALS

I. DIRECTIONS: In order to locate information in the library, it is important to be familiar with its organization. The nonfiction books are organized according to the Dewey Decimal System. Fill in the blanks next to each topic below with the appropriate Dewey Decimal numbers to indicate where in the library each can be found.

The Dewey Decimal System

000-099	General References	500-599	Science
100-199	Philosophy, Psychology	600-699	Applied Science, Technology
200-299	Religion	700-799	The Arts (music, art)
300-399	Social Science	800-899	Literature
400-499	Language	900-999	Geography/History

1. The Significance of Picasso's Painting *Guernica* _____
2. Why Volcanoes Erupt _____
3. Influences on the Poetry of Henry Wadsworth Longfellow _____
4. A Description of Buddhism _____
5. Sigmund Freud's Contributions to Modern Psychology _____

II. DIRECTIONS: The card catalog is an important tool for locating information in the library. All books found in the library are listed in the card catalog in three ways: by author, by title, and by subject. Cards in the catalog also contain the bibliographic information you will need later. When you first begin to research a subject, you will probably use the subject cards most. Later, your research will lead you to specific book titles and authors.

Under what subjects in the card catalog might you look to find information on the following? (Look for key words in the topics to help you.)

1. The Early Music of Mozart   _____ _____ _____

2. The Causes of the Civil War   _____ _____ _____

3. Black Holes in Space   _____ _____ _____

4. History of the World Series   _____ _____ _____

5. John F. Kennedy and the Bay of Pigs Invasion _____ _____ _____

 *ACTIVITY* **THREE**   *SELECTING APPROPRIATE*
REFERENCE MATERIALS

Directions:
One of the most important reference materials you will use when researching is the *Readers' Guide to Periodical Literature.* The *Readers' Guide* indexes over 125 periodicals (magazines). To use this tool, you need only look up the subject, author, or title of an article. The index will tell you the magazine, volume, date, and page number where the article can be found.

Using the *Readers' Guide,* identify the three best articles you might read to get information for each of the subjects listed below. For each article, list the following: author, title of article, name of magazine, date of publication, volume number, and page numbers.

1. Satellites and Television _____

_____

_____

_____

_____

2. Shoplifting _____

_____

_____

_____

_____

3. The Success of Lee Iacocca _____

_____

_____

_____

_____

4. The Conflict in Nicaragua _____

_____

_____

_____

_____

S T E P

3

SELECTING APPROPRIATE
REFERENCE MATERIALS ACTIVITY **FOUR**

Directions: Using the reference materials listed below, find the answers to the questions. After answering each, include the name of the reference book and the page number where your answer was found. Underline the key words in the questions to help you decide which reference book to use.

| Familiar Quotations | First Facts | Thesaurus | World Almanac |

World Atlas   *Current Biography Yearbook*   *Who's Who in America*

1. What was the most popular television program last year? _____

Reference _____ — Page _____

2. What would the weather be like in the Canary Islands in the month of December? _____

_____

Reference _____ Page _____

3. Find one quotation you like about the subject of "success." Copy the quotation and give its author.

_____

_____

Reference _____ Page _____

4. Find four synonyms for "success." _____

_____

Reference _____ Page _____

5. Who is your favorite living rock star? Find and list three interesting facts about this star.

_____

_____

Reference _____ Page _____

6. When was the first school in America established? _____

Reference _____ Page _____

NAME _____ DATE _____

ACTIVITY FIVE   *SELECTING APPROPRIATE REFERENCE MATERIALS*

Directions: When researching a subject, you need to decide what information you would like to discover in order to select the appropriate reference materials. For example, if you selected the subject "The Events Leading to Nathan Hale's Execution," you might want to know about Hale's personal values, the Revolutionary War, and any saying he is remembered for. In this example, you might want to consult the card catalog for nonfiction books on Hale and the Revolutionary War; *Webster's Biographical Dictionary* for additional information; and *Familiar Quotations* to learn of any quotations for which he might be remembered.

Using the subjects listed below, write three important aspects of this subject that should be considered in your investigation. Look over the list of reference materials on page 13 and decide which source(s) would best provide the information you are trying to find.

1. Subject: Computers and Education

What do you want to know?   *Reference materials*

a. _____   _____

b. _____   _____

c. _____   _____

2. Subject: Junk Food and You

What do you want to know?   *Reference materials*

a. _____   _____

b. _____   _____

c. _____   _____

3. Subject: Airline Safety

What do you want to know?   *Reference materials*

a. _____   _____

b. _____   _____

c. _____   _____

4. Subject: The Art of Andy Warhol

What do you want to know?   *Reference materials*

a. _____   _____

b. _____   _____

c. _____   _____

From *Take Ten . . . Steps to Successful Research*, Copyright © 1988 Scott, Foresman and Company.

ON YOUR OWN

Selecting Appropriate Reference Materials

You have already selected your focused subject for research. Now you need to select the sources that provide the *most relevant* information for this subject.

1. Decide what information you would like to discover concerning your subject. List these questions or ideas.

_____

_____

_____

_____

_____

2. Using the card catalog at your library, find the appropriate nonfiction books. After you have located these books, skim through them to see whether they provide the information you are seeking. For each that does, you will need to make a bibliography card. These cards will be of great value to you as you continue through the research steps.

To make bibliography cards, you will need 3 x 5 index cards to record information about each source you have selected. You should include the following information: name of author(s); title; place of publication; publisher; and date of publication. Below is an example of a bibliography card.

Meinbach, Anita Meyer, and Rothlein, Liz Christman.
Unlocking the Secrets of Research.
Glenview, Ill.: Scott, Foresman and Company, 1986.

Continued next page

3. Look up your subject in the *Readers' Guide to Periodical Literature*. Make up a bibliography card for each of the articles listed that you consider most relevant to your subject. The bibliography card for a periodical should include the following information: author; title of article; name of magazine; date of publication; page number(s).

4. Look over the reference materials listed on page 13. On the lines below, list those that would be most relevant to your subject. For any books you list, make bibliography cards.

_____

_____

_____

_____

_____

5. Keep your bibliography cards together in a file box or with rubber bands. As you begin your research, you may find that you will not use all of the sources. You may, however, find additional sources, which you may then add to your file.

REMINDER: Check off "Step 3: Select Appropriate Reference Materials" on your Student Checklist.

S T E P

4

Formulating a Thesis Statement

By now, you have focused your topic and selected the reference materials you feel will be most helpful. Before you continue, you need to clarify your purpose for doing the research. What is it you want to accomplish?

Writing a thesis statement will help you to keep your purpose in mind as you read and take notes. A "thesis" is simply a summary of the main idea or purpose of your research. As you write your thesis statement, keep the following in mind:

1. The thesis can take many forms. The thesis can be:
    a. a statement of your main idea.
    b. a statement of what you hope to learn.
    c. a statement of your opinion.
    d. a conclusion for which you hope to find support.

2. The thesis statement should be placed near the beginning of your research report to help you and your reader focus on the main idea of the research.

3. Make sure that what you are reading and taking notes on fit your thesis statement.

4. Make sure your paper has sufficient information to support your thesis statement. This information can be in the form of facts, examples, details, and so on.

Activity ONE *FORMULATING THE THESIS STATEMENT*

Directions: Look at the pictures below. Think about what is happening in each. Summarize the main idea of each picture by writing a short statement on the lines under each picture.

_____   _____

_____   _____

_____   _____

From *Distant Views,* p. 328, Copyright © 1987 Scott, Foresman and Company.

ACTIVITY TWO   *FORMULATING THE THESIS STATEMENT*

I. DIRECTIONS: Read the selections below. Create a title that best summarizes the content of each selection. Write this title on the line above each selection.

Title _____

People who have recently come to America might have trouble reading signs in English. But tired and hungry travelers would know which door to enter if they knew their word histories. The history of a word is its etymology. The etymology of a word tells what language the word came from and what the word meant in that language.

Restaurant comes from the French *restaurant* (res' tow ran') and can be traced back to the Latin *restaurare* (res' tou ra' ray), meaning "restore." If the travelers knew this, they would go into a restaurant to "restore their bodies."

Pharmacy comes from the Latin word *pharmacia* and can be traced back to Greek *pharmakon* (fär mä kone'), meaning "drug" or "medicine." If the travelers knew this, they would know to go to the pharmacy if they needed medicine.

Words that are derived from the same word and are spelled alike belong to the same *word family*. *Studio* comes from the Latin *studium* (stü' dee um), which means "to study." The words *student, study,* and *studious* also come from *studium* and all have to do with studying.

_____

From *Distant Views*, p. 302, Copyright © 1987 Scott, Foresman and Company.

Title _____

I think TV Turn Off Week is a good start toward solving the problem of TV mania. One week without TV may be enough to change bad viewing habits.

I am a TV buff. As soon as I wake up, I turn on the TV. Sometimes I even go to sleep to TV.

I watch exercise shows, even though I don't exercise. I once watched a show that taught typing, even though I don't own a typewriter.

My father is sympathetic to my problem. He said that when his family got their first TV, he and his brothers used to sit and watch *all* the commercials.

Anyway, my father has talked to me, and we've decided that one week without TV is a good beginning. If I can survive that week, I'll try to cut down on the amount of time that I watch TV from then on.

If there are any other TV buffs out there, try one week of no TV, too. It's going to be hard for me, but I am looking forward to building model planes. Maybe you, too, can look forward to enjoying a hobby.

_____

From *Distant Views*, p. 438, Copyright © 1987 Scott, Foresman and Company.

Continued next page

II. DIRECTIONS: Look at the selections on the preceding page. The main idea/purpose of the first one could be stated as "By tracing the history of many words in our language, we can discover that they originated from many other languages." This statement would be called the *thesis statement*. Read the selections below. Think about the main idea/purpose of each. Then summarize this main idea by writing a short statement (the thesis) on the lines under each selection.

The Dive
by Cornelia Brownell Gould

One moment, poised above the flashing blue:

The next I'm slipping, sliding through

The water that caresses, yields, resists,

Wrapping my sight in cooling grey-green mists

Another moment — and I swirl, I rise,

Shaking the water from my blinded eyes,

And strike out strong, glad that I am alive,

To swing back to the grey old pile from which I dive.

Someone You Should Know

Benito Juarez (ben ee' to whär' es) was a Zapotec (zä pe tek') Indian born in southern Mexico in 1806. He grew up on a farm and could not read or write until age twelve. It was then that a rich man took an interest in Juarez and sent him to school. Juarez never stopped learning.

Juarez became a lawyer, a judge, and in 1858 president of Mexico.

During the 1850s, Mexico was ruled by rich landowners. Revolutions raged all over the country. When Juarez became president, he vowed to reduce the power of the landowners and give the land back to the poor farmers.

For a while, Juarez made much progress. He reduced the power of the army and returned much farmland back to the poor people of the nation.

But then France invaded Mexico. Juarez was forced to flee his nation. But he was a Mexican citizen in the strongest sense of the word. He vowed to return and bring democracy to his beloved country.

In 1867, Juarez once again became president of Mexico. He hoped to build a huge school system to educate the people of his country. He knew that democracy would work only if the people were educated. Juarez had never forgotten how education had changed his life.

Despite his determination, Juarez never lived to see his dreams for his country come true. He died in 1872. For many years Mexico was run by one dictator after the other. Juarez's public school system was not realized for many years.

But Juarez's ideas about democracy lived on. Today, many of them are a part of Mexico's constitution.

From *Distant Views*, p. 244, Copyright © 1987 Scott, Foresman and Company.

ACTIVITY **THREE** *FORMULATING THE THESIS STATEMENT*

Directions: Think about your favorite television program and favorite movie. Based on your selections, complete the questions below.

Favorite television program _____

In one paragraph, summarize your favorite episode from this program.

_____

_____

_____

Write a brief statement to explain the purpose or main idea (the thesis) of the program.

_____

_____

_____

Favorite movie _____

In one paragraph, summarize this movie.

_____

_____

_____

Draw a picture to represent the main idea or purpose (the thesis) of this movie.

Based on the main idea or purpose of the movie, create a catchy new title:

_____

FORMULATING THE THESIS STATEMENT **ACTIVITY FOUR**

I. DIRECTIONS: Select an interesting article from your local newspaper. Read it and answer the following questions.

Name of newspaper _____

Headline _____

"Who" is the article about? _____

"What" happened? _____

"Where" and "When" did this happen? _____

"How" did this happen? _____

Based on the information in the article, what do you think the author's main idea/purpose was for writing it? (This would be the *thesis* for this article.)

_____

_____

_____

II. DIRECTIONS: Read an editorial in your local newspaper and answer the following questions.

Name of newspaper _____

Headline of editorial _____

Summary of the editorial _____

_____

_____

What facts/details/examples did the author use to back up his or her opinions? _____

_____

_____

Based on the information in the editorial, what do you think the author's main idea/purpose was for writing it? (This would be the *thesis* of the editorial.)

_____

_____

4

ACTIVITY **FIVE**   *FORMULATING THE THESIS STATEMENT*

Directions: Choose one of the topics in the box below. Read a general article related to the topic, write a summary of the article, and determine the author's thesis.

Athletes and Drugs   The Bermuda Triangle

Satellites and Communication

The Big Bang Theory

The Purposes of Totem Poles

The Limiting of Strategic Arms

Topic selected _____

Summary of article _____

_____

_____

_____

_____

Based on the information in the article, what do you think the main idea/purpose (the thesis) was?

_____

_____

_____

ON YOUR OWN

Formulating the Thesis Statement

Formulating the thesis statement is one of the most important steps in the research process. By carefully writing a good thesis statement, you will find it easier to keep the purpose of your research in mind as you read and take notes.

You have already focused the subject for your research and have identified several reference books that you feel will help you with your research. Now you must decide what the main idea/purpose (the thesis) of your research will be, based on your selected topic.

1. Skim through some of the reference materials you have selected. Carefully read *two* of the general articles and complete the questions below.

Title of Article #1 _____

Summary of Article #1 _____

_____

_____

_____

_____

What is the main idea/purpose (thesis) of this article? _____

_____

_____

Title of Article #2 _____

Summary of Article #2 _____

_____

_____

_____

_____

What is the main idea/purpose (thesis) of this article? _____

_____

_____

Continued next page

How were the purposes of the two articles alike? How were they different? _____

_____

_____

_____

_____

_____

2. Now you must decide on the main idea/purpose of your research. This will be *your* thesis. Do you want to summarize the information found on the subject? Do you want to offer an opinion and find information that supports (or perhaps refutes) this opinion? Do you want to state a conclusion and find information that supports (or perhaps refutes) this conclusion? Decide what you wish to do and write the thesis statement for your independent research project in the box below. Also, fill in the date and your signature.

The Thesis for My Research Will Be:

_____

_____

_____

_____

_____

_____

_____   _____
Signature   Date

REMINDER: Check off "Step 4: Formulate a Thesis Statement" on your Student Checklist.

GETTING STARTED

Writing the Outline

By now you have determined the main idea/purpose for your research and have written a thesis statement to explain it. You are now ready to organize the ideas and information you want to include in your research paper. To help with this organization, you will need an outline. The outline will insure that you have included everything you want to include, and it will help you to put this information in a logical order.

The following is an example of a simple outline and how information on the subject "Overweight" would fit this outline.

Outline Format

I. Main topic
  A. Subtopic
  B. Subtopic
  C. Subtopic
    1. Detail
    2. Detail
II. Main topic
  A. Subtopic
    1. Detail
    2. Detail
  B. Subtopic
  C. Subtopic
    1. Detail
    2. Detail

Example

I. Causes of overweight
  A. Slow metabolism
  B. Lack of exercise
  C. Poor eating habits
    1. Overeating
    2. Poor nutrition
II. Results of being overweight
  A. Medical problems
    1. High blood pressure
    2. Increased risk of heart attack
  B. Lethargy
  C. Poor self-concept
    1. Appearance
    2. Other perceptions

When writing an outline, it is important to remember the following:

1. An outline can be divided into main topics, subtopics, and details. The main topics tell the major points you want to include in your research paper. The subtopics explain something about the main topic. The details tell more about the subtopics.

2. Main topics are indicated with roman numerals (I, II, III, . . .). The subtopics are indicated by capital letters (A, B, C, . . .). The details are indicated by arabic numerals (1, 2, 3, . . .).

3. You should not have single subtopics or details. In other words, for every A you must have a B, and for every 1 you must have a 2.

4. In the outline above, notice how each of the details and subtopics have been indented. Use this format when preparing your outline.

5. The first word of each main topic, subtopic, and detail should begin with a capital letter.

From *Take Ten ...Steps to Successful Research*, Copyright © 1988, Scott, Foresman and Company.

ACTIVITY **ONE**   *WRITING THE OUTLINE*

Directions: Look at the words in the boxes. Decide which words are the main topics (main ideas) and which words are subtopics (supporting ideas that tell more about the main topic).

Archeological digs	Discovering prehistoric man	Making models of early man
How prehistoric man hunted	Studying fossils	

Main topic I. _____

Subtopics   A. _____

                  B. _____

                  C. _____

Main topic II. _____

Learning about different careers	-Education and training	Being interviewed
Choosing and planning for a career	Writing a resume	Applying for a job

Main topic I. _____

Subtopics   A. _____

                  B. _____

Main topic II. _____

                  A. _____

                  B. _____

Early experiments and ideas	History of the airplane	Fighter planes
Airplanes in war	First manned flights	Bombers

Main topic I. _____

Subtopic   A. _____

Subtopic   B. _____

Main topic II. _____

Subtopic   A. _____

Subtopic   B. _____

WRITING THE OUTLINE **ACTIVITY TWO**

Directions: Using the words/phrases in the boxes, fill in the outlines below by organizing the words/phrases into main topics, subtopics (which tell more about the main topics), and details (which tell more about the subtopics). Some of the entries have already been filled in.

The Moon

> What the moon is like, New moon,
> Mountains, The moon's surface,
> Quarter moon, Long narrow valleys, Orbit,
> How the moon moves, Full moon,
> Atmosphere and weather, Craters,
> Phases of the moon

I. What the moon is like

   A. _____

      1. _____

      2. _____

      3. _____

   B. _____

II. How the moon moves

   A. _____

   B. _____

      1. New moon

      2. _____

      3. _____

Camping

> Near firewood, Avoid sunburn, What to take,
> Clothing, Equipment, Making the camp,
> Pure drinking water, Near water,
> Nonperishable, Location, Washable,
> Health precautions, Food,
> Building a campfire, Comfortable,
> Identify poisonous plants

I. _____

   A. Equipment

   B. _____

      1. _____

      2. _____

   C. _____

      1. _____

      2. _____

II. Making the camp

   A. _____

      1. _____

      2. _____

   B. _____

III. _____

   A. Avoid sunburn

   B. _____

ACTIVITY THREE   *WRITING THE OUTLINE*

I. DIRECTIONS: Read the selection below and answer the questions that follow.

HANS CHRISTIAN ANDERSEN'S LIFE turned out to be like one of the fairy tales he is still remembered for. His family was very poor and lived in a one-room cottage. Andersen, at the age of fourteen, left his home town of Odense to seek his fortune in the theater in Copenhagen. He tried singing, acting, and dancing, but he was so unsuccessful that he almost starved.

An influential friend helped Andersen get a scholarship so that he could continue his education. After graduation, Andersen began a career of writing poems and novels and plays. But he wasn't successful in this either. Then he wrote four fairy tales and published them in a pamphlet, which was an immediate success.

While visiting a noble at the noble's country home, Andersen got to thinking about his life. Once he had been an ugly duckling in Odense and now he was like one of the swans that floated in the moat around the house. And so he wrote one of his most famous fairy tales, "The Ugly Duckling," which was really the story of his life.

From *Distant Views*, p. 141, Copyright © 1987 Scott, Foresman and Company.

1. What is the article about (main topic)?

   I. _____

2. Give two major points the article makes about this main topic (subtopics). For each subtopic, write two details to tell more about each.

   A. _____

      1. _____

      2. _____

   B. _____

      1. _____

      2. _____

NOTE: Keep this outline. You will need it for Step 7 Activity 2.

Continued next page

II. DIRECTIONS: Read the selection below and determine the main topics, the subtopics, and the details for each. Write these in correct outline form in the space below the article.

VIRGINIA HAMILTON GREW UP with her four brothers and sisters on a farm in Yellow Springs, Ohio. She was the youngest. Her brothers and sisters treated her with love, and her parents spoiled her. She often went to see cousins, aunts, and uncles who lived on neighboring farms. In looking back on her childhood, Hamilton considers herself fortunate to have been part of such a warm, loving extended family.

The author remembers her family as being great storytellers. No doubt they were an influence on her, because storytelling became her life's work.

The author's family helped to make the history of Yellow Springs, for they lived there for generations. The town of Yellow Springs played a part in the history of the United States. It was a station on the Underground Railway, and many of the people living there today are descendants of abolitionists and fugitive slaves. The Underground Railway was a source of inspiration to Hamilton for a book called *The House of Dies Drear*. It tells about an old house that was used as a shelter by the people who ran the Underground Railroad. The book was later made into a TV movie.

The author still lives in Yellow Springs on land that was once part of the farm on which she grew up.

Hamilton's book *M. C. Higgins, the Great* received the Newbery Award and the National Book Award in 1975. Many of her other books have received awards, too.

From *Distant Views*, p. 356, Copyright © 1987 Scott, Foresman and Company.

_____

_____

_____

_____

_____

_____

_____

_____

_____

_____

_____

_____

_____

_____

ACTIVITY FOUR   *WRITING THE OUTLINE*

Directions:
Imagine that you were writing a research paper on the subject "UFOs" (Step 1). After narrowing the subject (Step 2), you decided to research the subject "UFO Sitings." To help you select the appropriate reference materials (Step 3), you came up with the following questions/ideas that you wanted to cover in your research:

1. Where have UFOs been seen?
2. Do UFOs really exist?
3. How do scientists explain UFO sitings?
4. How do scientists investigate UFO sitings?
5. What equipment is used to investigate UFO sitings?
6. Can all sitings be explained by science?

After reading several general articles related to UFO sitings, you decided on the following thesis (Step 4) for your research: "Over the years, many UFOs have been sited. Often science and scientists can explain these sitings, but there are some UFO sitings that remain a mystery."

To help you organize your research, you now need to write an outline. What other questions/ideas do you feel would be important to cover on "UFO Sitings"?

_____   _____

_____   _____

_____   _____

Look over the list you have just written and look at the six ideas/questions listed for Step 3. Decide which ideas would be main topics, which would be subtopics to explain the main topics, and which would be details, which tell more about the subtopics. Now create an outline for the research paper on "UFO Sitings."

_____

_____

_____

_____

_____

_____

_____

_____

   From *Take Ten . . . Steps to Successful Research,* Copyright © 1988 Scott, Foresman and Company.

Writing the Outline

ON YOUR OWN

To help with the organization of your research paper, it is important to prepare an outline. The outline will help you be sure that you have included everything you want to include and will help you put this information in a logical order.

1. Write the subject you chose for your own independent research (Step 1):

_____

2. When you focused your subject (Step 2), what topic did you choose?

_____

3. For Step 3, you listed questions/ideas you wanted to cover in your research. List these questions/ideas below:

_____

_____

_____

4. Write the thesis statement you developed in Step 4 on the lines below:

_____

_____

_____

5. Now that you have read several articles relating to your subject, what other questions/ideas do you feel would be important to cover in your research?

_____   _____

_____   _____

_____   _____

Continued next page

6. Look over the list you have just written and look at the questions/ideas you listed in #3 on the previous page. Decide which ideas would be main topics, which would be subtopics to explain the main topics, and which would be details, which tell more about the subtopics. Create an outline for your independent research. Put this outline in the box below. Also fill in the date and your signature.

Outline for (Subject) _____

_____

_____

_____

_____

_____

_____

_____

_____

_____

_____

_____

_____

_____

_____

_____

_____

_____   _____
Signature   Date

REMINDER: Check off "Step 5: Write an Outline" on your Student Checklist.

From *Take Ten . . . Steps to Successful Research*, Copyright © 1988 Scott, Foresman and Company.

Preparing Note Cards and Taking Notes

You are now halfway through the research process! You are ready to read the reference material you selected and to take notes. It is important that you take notes that are accurate and concise (brief and to the point), since these notes will become the backbone of your research paper. When taking notes, the following ideas will be helpful:

1. Not all the reference materials you found will be appropriate. Establish reasons for selecting the *best sources*.

    a. Consider the publication date of each reference source. For example, you would not want to use a book published in 1950 for research on the subject of space travel. However, a book written in 1950 might be acceptable if your research focused on the first horseless carriages (automobiles). The best rule would be to obtain the most recently published materials.

    b. Make sure the source is reliable. Is the information accurate (true)? Some authors will try to make you believe their point of view by manipulating (controlling) the statistics, dates, or other facts. For example, an author may include only those statistics or facts that support a personal belief and ignore findings that do not.

    c. Decide whether the source has the information necessary to develop the thesis (main idea/purpose) you wrote.

2. Do not copy everything! Write down main ideas, putting them into your own words. Think about what you are reading and then summarize it. When you find you *must* copy something exactly, you will have to use quotation marks and indicate the source and page number where the quotation can be found.

3. Include ideas in your notes that might not seem to agree. You will need to know everything you can concerning your subject. This will enable you to form your own conclusions.

4. Take notes as you read. Keep your outline in mind as you take notes, and try to find information to cover the main topics and subtopics.

5. When taking notes, you should put all information discovered on note cards. A detailed explanation for preparing note cards appears on pages 45–46.

ACTIVITY **ONE**   *PREPARING NOTE CARDS*
                   AND TAKING NOTES

Directions: When taking notes, it is important to be able to recognize whether the information is "fact" or "opinion." A "fact" is something that can be *proven* to be true. An "opinion" is something that cannot be proven and is often simply based on a person's point of view. For example, the statement "Palm trees grow in Florida" is a fact. It can be proven. The statement "Palm trees are one of the most beautiful trees in Florida" is an opinion. This statement cannot be proven.

Read the following statements. Place the word "fact" by those statements that can be proven, and place the word "opinion" by those that cannot be proven.

1. _____ Vermont is a state in the northeastern United States.

2. _____ Actresses are always beautiful.

3. _____ All decisions made by our Presidents are made for the good of the country.

4. _____ Wendy's makes the best hamburgers.

5. _____ Canada is the world's second largest country in land size.

6. _____ The largest mammal is the blue whale.

7. _____ Space travel is too dangerous for most people.

8. _____ Every country has its own system of money.

9. _____ The most accurate method of measurement is the metric system.

10. _____ All Democrats are more liberal (tolerant, broad-minded) than Republicans.

11. _____ The most perfect time to visit Switzerland is during the fall months.

12. _____ The mythology of ancient cultures helps us to understand many things about life at that time.

On the lines below, write two facts about yourself:

_____   _____

On the lines below, write two opinion statements about yourself:

_____   _____

Look over the fact and opinion statements on this page. Often, there are words that provide clues to help you identify those statements that are opinions, such as "always," "most," and "best." Go back and underline these and other such words in the statements you identified as being opinion.

PREPARING NOTE CARDS
AND TAKING NOTES ACTIVITY TWO

Directions: To write note cards, it is important to be able to select the main ideas from what you are reading. In addition, you need to be able to summarize these main ideas in your own words and in a concise way (brief and to the point). Remember, you *can't* copy everything you read on your subject.

Read the selection below and answer the questions following it. This will help you to select and summarize the main ideas.

Far Out Farms
by Lisa Hsia

THE WORLD'S POPULATION is growing fast. Today there are 4-1/2 billion people in the world. By the time you become thirty, there will be 6-1/2 billion. These people will take up much of the earth's food-growing space. Therefore, new places and ways have to be found to grow enough healthful food to feed the world's increasing population.

Perhaps the food in your future will be grown with the help of computers or strange potions. Greenhouses might help future farmers grow food in deserts, under the sea, or even in space. Some foods might not resemble anything you eat today. Food may never be the same again.

Imagine a farm with rows and rows of plants. They stretch as far as the eye can see. A farmer drives a mechanical harvester through the field gathering the crop. It sounds like a pretty normal scene — until you learn that the farm is underwater!

Of course, farmers aren't driving harvesters on the ocean floor right now. But farming is already going on in the sea. Someday, when people settle on dry land now used for growing food, underwater farms could come in handy.

Today's underwater farming, called aquaculture, is not a big business. People are growing sea plants such as kelp and algae in small, offshore water fields in California and Japan. Some people eat the high-protein plants. Kelp is even used as an ingredient in some ice creams. Some day there could be huge farms on the sea floor. They could grow hundreds of thousands of acres of plants for food and fuel.

There's another kind of underwater farming being done now that isn't farming plants. It's farming fish! Salmon ranchers grow fish in pens that float in the sea. Some shellfish, such as clams, grow from ropes dangling into the water from floats. Lobsters are also raised in underwater cages.

"Aquaculture accounts for 11 percent of the fish eaten in the United States," says Peter Cook, an aquaculture expert. Therefore, there's a good chance that some of the fish you eat already comes from a fish farm.

Reproduced by permission of Children's Television Workshop.

Continued next page

What is the main reason for needing "Far Out Farms"? _____

_____

How and where might food be grown in the future? _____

_____

What are some things that could be grown underwater? _____

_____

What new terms might be created as a result of "Far Out Farms"? _____

_____

Write a summary of the main ideas of this selection. Be as brief as possible. _____

_____

_____

_____

*PREPARING NOTE CARDS
AND TAKING NOTES*   ACTIVITY **THREE**

Directions: Read the selection below and think about the main ideas the article presents. Ask yourself questions about the article to help better understand what you have read. (Look at the questions on the previous page and see how they helped you to identify the main ideas.) On the lines below the article, write a brief summary of the main ideas presented.

Life on a Space Shuttle
by Bruce Meberg

THE CHANCES THAT YOU MAY ONE DAY take a trip into space are getting better all the time. As it becomes easier to live in a space capsule, more and more people who are *not* trained astronauts will be able to travel in space. At first, the National Aeronautics and Space Administration (NASA) would only choose as astronauts trained pilots to carry out the early space programs. These were the Mercury and Gemini programs. For the Apollo and Skylab flights, doctors and scientists were added to the list of those able to take part in space flights.

A space shuttle crew may number up to seven people. The commander, the pilot, and the mission specialist are NASA astronauts. Other people in the crew are called *payload specialists*. They may or may not be NASA astronauts. Payload specialists are people who are already trained in special scientific or medical skills. They are taken along on spaceflights to carry out the scientific and medical experiments of a mission. What special skills of your chosen career might be useful on a space shuttle mission? This is where your chance to travel in space might be.

Today, choosing candidates for space travel is still hard to do, but the Space Shuttle Program has made some of its requirements easier to meet. Now, ordinary people are sometimes able to take part in a space flight. Through NASA's Space Flight Participant Program politicians and other civilians have had their chance. One day, you, too, may be able to travel into outer space.

As the dream of space flight becomes real for more and more people, you may wonder, "What might a space flight be like? How is life in a space capsule different from life on Earth?"

From *Distant Views*, pp. 474–475, Copyright © 1987 Scott, Foresman and Company.

_____

_____

_____

6

ACTIVITY **FOUR**   *PREPARING NOTE CARDS AND TAKING NOTES*

Directions: It is very important to find evidence to support the statements you are making. The evidence you find can take many forms, such as facts (something that is true that can be proven); quotations (statements made by experts); and statistics (facts and figures which are numerical).

Read the selction below, then answer the questions. On the blank before each question, tell whether the answer is a fact, quotation, or statistic.

Working to Solve Environmental Problems

Environmental problems are not new. But many problems are worse now than ever before. Why?

One reason is the increased population. More people live on the earth today than at any time in the past. More people means more pollutants are added to the air, water, and land. More people means more noise is made. And more people means natural resources are used up faster.

In addition, certain advances in technology have made some environmental problems worse. For example, modern technology involves the production of many chemical wastes. Some chemical wastes are dangerous pollutants. Completely safe ways to dispose of these wastes have not yet been developed.

Today's environmental problems are very serious. But many of them can be solved. It is important to try to solve them because a healthy environment can greatly benefit physical, mental, and social health.

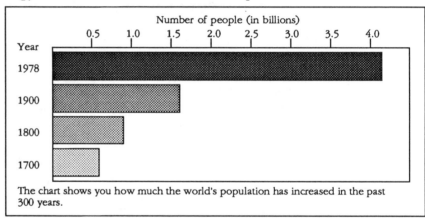

The chart shows you how much the world's population has increased in the past 300 years.

From *Choosing Good Health*, grade 6, p. 255, by Merita Lee Thompson, et al., Copyright © 1983 Scott, Foresman and Company.

1. _____ How much did the world population increase from 1900 to 1978? _____

2. _____ Give one reason to explain why environmental problems are worse now than ever before.

_____

3. _____ Between which years has the world's population grown the most? _____

4. _____ How has technology made our environmental problems worse? _____

_____

Using other sources, find one quotation that relates to the environment. Write the quotation. List the reference (source title, author of quote, page).

_____

_____

STEP 6

*PREPARING NOTE CARDS
AND TAKING NOTES*   **ACTIVITY FIVE**

Directions: Read the selection titled "Storm Chasers." Following the selection are note cards, each relating to a different topic concerning tornadoes. Using the information from the article, summarize the main ideas for each topic and put these notes on the correct cards. Also, include facts and statistics (details) that you feel best support the main idea you summarized, and put this information on the correct note cards. Indicate the page numbers for any statistics and quotations you use, and be sure to put quotation marks around quotations or anything you copy word-for-word.

Storm Chasers
by Marion Long

Most of the storm chasers in the United States work with either the National Severe Storm Laboratory in Norman, Oklahoma, or with the Institute for Disaster Research at Texas Tech University in Lubbock. The scientists in Oklahoma and Texas keep looking at the local radar scans and the other latest facts to pinpoint the chase for their people in the field. But not David Hoadley.

Hoadley chases storms on his own. He uses only the information given to anyone who walks into a U.S. Weather Service station. And while the chasers at the Severe Storm Lab or at Texas Tech can chase storms anytime, for Hoadley, tornado season is his yearly three-week vacation. Most of the year he works as a budget analyst for the Environmental Protection Agency. But in May he heads for the Great Plains. He watches the stretch of land from Texas to Iowa known as Tornado Alley — states most often hit by tornadoes yearly. Usually he travels alone, but once he allowed this reporter to go with him.

We headed toward the west Texas panhandle, Hoadley's choice. He explained to me that scientists aren't exactly sure of how tornadoes are born, but they know what weather conditions come before them. All it takes is an area of warm air filled with moisture and an area of cold, heavy air above it, preventing its efforts to rise.

At some spot in the layer, warm air escapes and the cold air moves down. The rising warm air gives the falling cold air a high-speed spin. As the atmosphere struggles to adjust, a vortex of currents is created. The air begins spinning, forms a column, and falls downward. Low pressure within the vortex causes water vapor to condense, so that the tornado can be seen. That low pressure also causes a pull upward. Chickens have had all of their feathers pulled. Cars, houses, and bridges have been picked up and moved. So have people.

Here, on the plains of western Texas, there were no tornadoes in sight. It was very hot, and the car was not air-conditioned. Because we had no luck that day, we drove on to Kansas. In the morning, at the weather station, Hoadley had happily drawn a big lemon-shaped storm-watch circle from Wichita to Salina. Most tornadoes develop along a boundary between cool dry air from the north and warm, humid air from the Gulf of Mexico. It was 38 degrees in Cook, Nebraska, and it would reach the 70s in Kansas. We sat in the car on a deserted road, looking at stormy clouds that were ragged with turning. (On a normal weather day, the bottoms of fluffy, cumulus clouds are flat.) We listened to the eerie wind in the power lines.

Because we had no luck in Kansas, we drove south to the weather station in Hobart, Oklahoma. We found that this was what was called a high-risk day for storm activity — a very rare occurrence.

In the car, Hoadley was lost in thought and very happy. He let out a yell and began to shoot pictures of huge, hard, well-defined clouds. As we drove, conditions changed amazingly fast. Even in the short time between picture stops, the sky was being rearranged.

A twenty-foot curtain of dust blew thick across the highway. "There go the tumbleweeds," shouted Hoadley. Bunches of them went rolling across the road before the wind.

Continued next page

Then, suddenly, all was sunlight and chirping birds. Hoadley got out of the car and pointed his arm west. The storm was picking up again. Now the clouds were moving very quickly. The trees were defying the strong gusting winds that rocked the car.

"This is the kind of storm that takes seventy-ton boxcars and lifts them off the tracks," Hoadley said. He followed this observation with a few short instructions about how to survive in a ditch if we had to leave the car. The tops of the clouds were rounding and getting tighter. It was nearly sunset, it became almost calm again for a minute. Hoadley was relaxed enough to begin talking about the kinds of birds you hear at sunset. Then a huge blue tornado dropped out of the sky. Like a snake, it whipped through space, slithering along for miles. But it was duller and heavier than a snake. It was like a wavy pillar of smoke. As the seconds went by, it seemed to grow in size until it was huge and black. The tornado picked at the fields and sucked

huge pieces up, spinning them in the darkness. The winds were moaning, almost howling. We had made the good forecast and had found the storm.

Then there was stillness on the plains. The whole world seemed to glow. There was great fear associated with the thing. As it pushed toward us, it seemed to wind like a smoky veil.

But the path of a tornado is no place for sitting and thinking. Hoadley suddenly threw up his hands in panic. A camera lens banged to the ground. He put the car into motion. "If you can't see the cloud and ground in the camera's viewfinder," said Hoadley, "or if you can hear the roar of the funnel, then you're too close." He looked back to see the tornado across the field behind, and he continued to drive away from the storm.

This tornado was later classified as the largest one that day, about 500 yards wide. It cut a path for seventeen miles behind where we first saw it touch down.

What Causes Tornadoes
Long, Marion. "Storm Chasers"

Damages of Tornadoes
Long, Marion. "Storm Chasers"

What a Tornado Is Like
Long, Marion. "Storm Chasers"

From *Take Ten . . . Steps to Successful Research*, Copyright © 1988 Scott, Foresman and Company.

ON YOUR OWN

Preparing Note Cards and Taking Notes

Congratulations! You are now halfway through the research process for your own independent project. Now it's time to read the reference materials you identified in Step 3 and take notes. These notes will help you to write your research paper and, if done correctly, will make this writing easy.

All notes you take should be written on note cards. Note cards will help you organize your information. The following steps describe how note cards are written:

1. You will need either 4 x 6 or 3 x 5 index cards.

2. Write a heading on each note card. The heading will be the subtopics you wrote in your outline (Step 5).

3. Use only one side of each note card, and don't try to put too much information on one card.

4. Put information from one book only on each card. Therefore, you will need several cards for each subtopic.

5. As you read a book and find information relating to one of the subtopics, *summarize the information* on the appropriate note card. If you find important information that doesn't fit your outline but fits your thesis, simply make out a card with a new heading.

6. Put the name of the author and title of the source on each card. (The other information you will need is already on the bibliography cards you wrote.)

7. Put the page numbers from which any statistics or quotations are taken.

Sample Note Card:

Heading, based on outline ——————— **I. Causes of overweight**
C.   Poor eating habits

Author and source ——————— Smith, John. *Nutrition Today*

Quotation and page number ——————— "_____" p. 27

Continued next page

Sample Note Card:

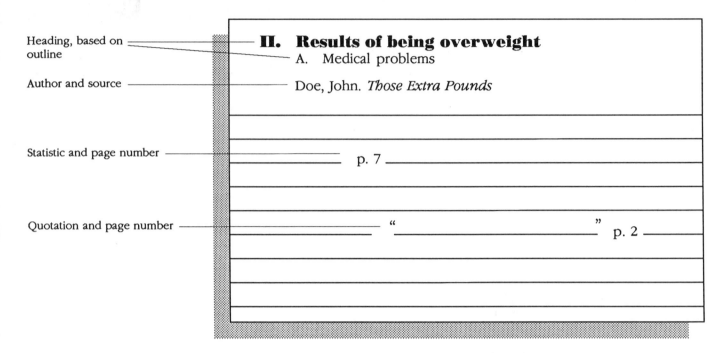

Heading, based on outline

Author and source

Statistic and page number

Quotation and page number

II. Results of being overweight
A. Medical problems

Doe, John. *Those Extra Pounds*

p. 7

" " p. 2

Take out the bibliography cards you wrote for Step 3 and begin to collect your reference materials. Look through them and choose the best materials to use for your research. When deciding which materials are best, you need to consider the publishing date, the reliability of the source, and whether it has the information you will need to develop the ideas in the thesis statement you wrote and in the outline you developed.

Prepare note cards for your independent research based on your outline. Remember to prepare several cards for each subtopic. Keep your note cards together in a file box so that none of them get lost.

Now you are ready to take notes. Remember, do not copy everything — just *main ideas* and the facts, statistics, and quotations (details) needed to support these ideas.

REMINDER: Check off "Step 6: Prepare Note Cards and Take Notes" on your Student Checklist.

Revising the Outline

The outline serves many important purposes. Besides helping organize your research, the outline can help you determine what information is missing from your notes. By comparing your outline to the notes you have already taken, you can easily learn what additional information you will have to locate.

Often, based on your note taking, it will become necessary to revise your outline. The following situations would cause you to revise your outline:

1. Finding material that doesn't fit your outline but is important to the subject. In this case, you will have to add main topics, subtopics, or details to your outline.

2. Finding no material that fits certain main topics, subtopics, or details in the outline. In this case, you will have to delete the items from your outline.

3. Finding you have single subtopics or single details. Remember, for every A you must have a B and for every 1 you must have a 2.

When revising your outline, remember that it is one of the most important tools in the research process. Feel free to make changes in your outline. You do not need to stay with your original outline if it is not appropriate for the information you have located. Change it to meet the needs of your research.

S T E P

7

NAME   DATE

ACTIVITY ONE   *REVISING THE OUTLINE*

Directions: Review the rules for writing an outline:

1. For every subtopic A there must be a B.

2. For every detail 1 there must be a 2.

3. Main topics must be indicated with roman numerals (I, II, III, . . .).

4. Subtopics must be indicated with capital letters (A, B, C, . . .).

5. Details must be indicated with arabic numerals (1, 2, 3, . . .).

6. Subtopics and details should be indented.

7. The first word of each main topic, subtopic, and detail must begin with a capital letter.

Look at the outlines below. Each outline has at least one error. Determine what changes need to be made and write the outline correctly in the space to the right of the original outline. There may be times that you will have to reword a subtopic or main topic. For example, if you have an A and no B, you will have to either delete the A and incorporate its idea into the larger main topic or create a B.

Mythology

I. What myths are about
   1. Mythical beings
   2. Mythical places
   3. Mythical symbols
II. Greek mythology
   1. The creation myth
   2. Greek divinities
   3. Greek heroes
III. Roman mythology
   1. Roman divinities
     a. Jupiter
   2. Roman heroes

Mythology

Lyndon Baines Johnson

I. Early life
   A. Boyhood
II. Early political career
   A. entry into politics
   B. youth administrator
III President, 1963–1969
   A. Assassination of President Kennedy
   B. Problems as president
     1. Foreign policy

Lyndon Baines Johnson

REVISING THE OUTLINE ACTIVITY **TWO**

Directions: Based on the information you were provided, you have already written an outline on Hans Christian Andersen (Step 5 Activity 3). Pretend you have done further research and have taken additional notes on Hans Christian Andersen. You find these notes do not fit into the outline you wrote but would be important facts to cover in a research paper on his life. Using these notes, *revise* your outline by adding main topics, subtopics, and/or details to your original outline. Write your revised outline on the lines provided and be sure to use the rules for correctly writing outlines.

Additional Notes on Andersen

1. Some of Andersen's best-loved fairy tales include "The Tinderbox," "Little Claus and Big Claus," and "The Traveling Companion."

2. Several tales were based on his life. These tales include "The Ugly Duckling" and "She Was Good for Nothing."

3. Several of Andersen's tales were about Denmark.

4. Several of his tales made fun of human faults, including "The Emperor's New Clothes" and "The Rags."

5. He never married but fell in love with three different women, including Jenny Lind, the famous singer.

6. He became friends with royalty and fellow artists, such as the composer Franz Liszt and the poet Heinrich Heine.

7. He wrote an autobiography titled *The Fairy Tale of My Life*.

Hans Christian Andersen

_____   _____
_____   _____
_____   _____
_____   _____
_____   _____
_____   _____
_____   _____
_____   _____
_____   _____
_____   _____
_____   _____

ACTIVITY THREE   *REVISING THE OUTLINE*

Directions: Pretend you have just completed writing the outline on "Knights" that is provided below. You then took notes using sources you had identified earlier. When you compared your original outline with the notes you took, you located the following problems:

1. One of the sources you found contained the article "Training to Be a Knight" (included on the following page). You found this information to be very important to your subject. However, your outline made no reference to this information.

2. You were unable to find any information on the subtopic "Origin of tournaments."

3. You were unable to find any information on the detail "Pauldrons."

Based on this new information, *revise* the outline.

Knights

I. Clothing
   A. Sleeved undertunic
      1. Wool
      2. Linen
   B. Stockings and leather shoes
   C. Fur-lined long-sleeved coat with hood

II. Armor
   A. Conical helmet
   B. Mail—garment with metal rings
   C. Pauldrons—plates of metal
   D. Gauntlets—metal gloves

III. Tournaments
   A. Origin of tournaments
      1. When
      2. Where
   B. Rules
      1. Governing game
      2. Consequences of breaking rules—imprisonment and loss of property
   C. Events of tournaments
      1. Jousting
      2. Tilting
   D. Weapons

Continued next page

     From *Take Ten . . . Steps to Successful Research*, Copyright © 1988 Scott, Foresman and Company.

Training to Be a Knight

The Page's Training

To be a knight required that you start young, for you had many things to learn, not simply about warfare but about courtesy as well. The son of a knight might be taken from the care of his mother as early as seven years of age and sent off to the castle of some powerful nobleman to begin his training as a page. Every kind of menial job was his: fetching and carrying, running errands, helping the lady of the household in all her many duties, learning to come when he was called and to wait patiently when there was nothing for him to do. As he grew older, his day filled. He might be taught to play some musical instrument, to compose verse, and to wait on table. He learned the use of arms—the sword, the lance, the axe, on which his life would someday depend—and he practiced wrestling, leaping, running, and vaulting into the saddle without touching the stirrup while in full armor. All this training prepared him for the next step: to become a squire, at about the age of fourteen.

The Squire's Tasks

And now there were still other details of service to learn and perform. As a squire he had to know how to carve every sort of meat at the table and to know the correct word for each type of carving. A deer was *broken*, a swan was *lifted*, a hen was *despoiled*, a duck was *unbraced*, and a peacock was *disfigured*. He had to know every aspect of the hunt, with the right words to describe a *skulk* of foxes, a *sounder* of swine, or a *pride* of lions; he had to be familiar with the care and repairing of armor, with the management of hounds, with the mews where the hawks were trained. As squire of the bedchamber he must help his lord undress, comb his hair, prepare his bed, and even "drive out the dog and cat, giving them a clout." As squire of the body he must keep his lord's weapons and armor in good condition, replacing worn leather and burnishing away rust; as squire of the stables he must groom and exercise horses and learn how to train a warhorse; as squire of the table he must cut bread, pour beverages, and serve properly with a napkin over his arm.

Revised Outline: Knights

_____   _____

_____   _____

_____   _____

_____   _____

_____   _____

_____   _____

_____   _____

_____   _____

_____   _____

_____   _____

Revising the Outline

ON YOUR OWN

Now that you have taken notes on the subject you selected for your independent research, it is time to take a look at how well your notes fit the outline you created in Step 5. It will probably be necessary for you to revise your original outline to fit the information you found, as well as the information you were unable to locate.

1. Compare the completed note cards with your original outline. On the lines below, list the subtopics and details for which you were unable to locate information:

_____   _____

_____   _____

_____   _____

_____   _____

2. Search for additional sources that could provide the information you need for these subtopics and details. Take notes on the appropriate note cards.

3. Cross out the subtopics and details from the outline for which you still cannot locate information.

4. Compare your note cards and outline again. This time, look for notes on any main topics, subtopics, or details that were *not* included in your outline but that you feel are important to your research paper. Add these to your original outline.

5. Analyze your outline. Are the main topics, subtopics, and details in the order you would like to follow when you write your research paper? If not, you will need to rearrange the order of your outline.

6. Write your revised outline on the next page. Remember, you may have to reword your main topics, subtopics, and details based on the information you added and/or deleted. Also fill in your signature and the date.

Continued next page

Revised Outline for (Subject) _____

_____

_____

_____

_____

_____

_____

_____

_____

_____

_____

_____

_____

_____

_____

_____

_____   _____

Signature   Date

REMINDER: Check off "Step 7: Revise the Outline" on your Student Checklist.

Writing the First Draft

Now that you have revised your outline based on the notes you've taken, it's time to begin writing your research paper. As with any other type of writing, it is important to write a draft. A first draft gives you the opportunity to put down all your thoughts and ideas without worrying about mistakes in spelling, grammar, or punctuation. Later, you will have the opportunity to make any necessary changes. The following ideas will help you as you write your first draft:

1. Organize your note cards according to your revised outline. Put the note cards out on a table and categorize them by the subtopics. Next place the note cards for each subtopic in order according to the outline. Number the cards once they are in the correct order, by placing a number in the lower righthand corner

2. To help you organize your thoughts and ideas, keep your outline handy as you begin to write the first draft.

3. As you write the first draft, it is best to put away the resources you used. Instead, rely on the notes you took and on your outline. This will prevent you from being tempted to copy material from the resources.

4. Often, you will discover that similar information appears on several cards. You will have to decide how to combine this information rather than simply repeat it.

5. As you write your first draft, skip two lines between each line. This will make it easier to make revisions.

6. Once you begin writing, any questions you have about spelling or other possible errors should be noted in the margin. Later you can go back and check these errors, but for now you don't want to interrupt the flow of ideas as you write.

7. If you use a direct quotation or statistic, write down the page number and source in the margin next to the information. This will help you compile your footnotes when you write your final draft.

8. Make sure to put your thesis statement in the first paragraph. As you write the first draft, include all information to support this statement.

9. Write an introduction that includes your thesis statement. Your introduction should also point out the importance of your research or the reasons you selected this particular subject. Remember that your introduction needs to capture the attention of the audience and make them want to read more.

10. Your conclusion should be a brief summary of the ideas you have included in the body of the paper. In the conclusion you have the opportunity to include your own ideas based on the information found.

ACTIVITY**ONE**   *WRITING THE FIRST DRAFT*

I. DIRECTIONS: The information on your note cards describes the subtopics and details in your outline. It is easier to write a first draft when you put the note cards in order according to the outline. Using the outline provided, organize and number each note card below. Place the number of the card on the line in the lower righthand corner. (Note: Cards are not provided for every subtopic.)

Activities and Careers of the Police

I.   Police activities
    A.   Patrol operations
        1.   Beats
        2.   Arrests
    B.   Traffic operations
        1.   Promote safety
        2.   Direct traffic
        3.   Parking enforcement
II. Police careers
    A.   City police
    B.   County police
    C.   State police

I.   Police activities
    A.   Patrol operations

Craig, Ron. *Police Work*

Police can arrest a person they see committing a crime or have reasonable cause to suspect.

I.   Police activities
    A.   Patrol operations

Doe, John. *The Police*

In some cases, police are required to get a court order, called a traffic warrant, before making an arrest.

I.   Police activities
    B.   Traffic operations

Doe, John. *The Police*

Some departments use helicopters to survey and direct traffic.

I.   Police activities
    A.   Patrol operations

Brown, Joe. *Squad Cars*

Patrol officers are assigned areas or routes to cover on foot, horseback, squad cars, or on motorcycles.

I.   Police activities
    B.   Traffic operations

Smith, Jan. *Investigations*

Officers investigate traffic accidents and enforce speed limits.

Continued next page

II. DIRECTIONS: Now that you have numbered your cards, write two paragraphs to develop the subtopics on the note cards.

Patrol operations:

_____

_____

_____

_____

_____

_____

Traffic operations:

_____

_____

_____

_____

_____

_____

_____

_____

ACTIVITY **TWO** | *WRITING THE FIRST DRAFT*

Directions: When writing the first draft for a research paper, you may discover that similar information appears on several note cards. You will have to decide how to combine this information rather than simply repeat it. Below is a partial outline on the subject "Motion Pictures," as well as several note cards on the subtopic "Entertainment" and the detail "Enjoyment." Write a paragraph combining the information found on the note cards. If you use a quotation or statistic, indicate the source and page number in the margin.

I.   Importance of motion pictures
   A.   Entertainment
      1.   Escape
      2.   Enjoyment
   B.   Education and information
      1.   Classroom use
      2.   Government use

I.   Importance of motion pictures
   A.   Entertainment

Roth, Ash. *Memorable Movies*

People enjoy movies for many reasons. They may like the humor, the actors in the movie, or the plot.

Write your paragraph on the lines below.

_____

_____

_____

_____

_____

_____

_____

I.   Importance of motion pictures
   A.   Entertainment

Beck, Jay. *At the Movies*

While watching a movie, people like to try to figure out what will happen next and later discuss this plot with their friends.

I.   Importance of motion pictures
   A.   Entertainment

Kim, Terry. *Suspense in Movies*

One of the most popular types of movies is mysteries. People love the suspense of a good mystery.

I.   Importance of motion pictures
   A.   Entertainment

Davids, Kenneth. *Why Watch?*

"The motion picture is one of the most popular forms of entertainment in the U.S." p. 6. Movies can be funny, exciting, and adventuresome.

WRITING THE FIRST DRAFT ACTIVITY THREE

I. DIRECTIONS: Pretend you are going to write a research paper on the subject "Floods." Using the subtopics and details provided in the outline below, write a thesis statement, an introduction, and a conclusion.

Floods

I.   Effect of a flood
    A.   Destroys homes and property
        1.   Water damage
        2.   Force of water collapses property
    B.   Causes injuries and deaths

II. Causes of floods
    A.   Melting snow and ice
    B.   Heavy rains
    C.   Poor drainage

III. Preventing floods
    A.   Planting trees
    B.   Structures
        1.   Reservoirs
        2.   Dams
        3.   Levees

Thesis statement (write a summary of the main idea or the purpose of your research):

_____

_____

_____

_____

_____

_____

_____

_____

Introduction (write an interesting, creative, and attention-getting introduction that includes your thesis statement):

_____

_____

_____

_____

_____

_____

_____

_____

_____

_____

Continued next page

From *Take Ten . . . Steps to Successful Research*, Copyright © 1988, Scott, Foresman and Company.

Conclusion (be sure to briefly review or summarize the ideas that are included in the body of the paper):

_____

_____

_____

II. DIRECTIONS: Compare the thesis statement, introduction, and conclusion you have written with those written by at least two other students in the class, then answer the following:

1. What did the others state as their thesis (main idea/purpose) for the paper?

_____

_____

_____

2. Which of the introductions did you find to be most interesting? What about it made it so interesting? (Be specific.)

_____

_____

_____

3. Which of the conclusions did you find to be the best written? Explain the reasons that made it a good conclusion.

_____

_____

_____

4. What have you learned about writing introductions?

_____

_____

5. What have you learned about writing conclusions?

_____

_____

_____

From *Take Ten . . . Steps to Successful Research*, Copyright © 1988 Scott, Foresman and Company.

STEP 8

WRITING THE FIRST DRAFT ACTIVITY **FOUR**

Directions: Pretend that you are writing a research paper based not only on the outline below but on one of the purposes (your thesis) listed in the box. Write a creative introduction for this paper that will grab the attention of the reader and that includes a statement of the thesis. Write a conclusion that will provide a brief summary. In the conclusion you have the opportunity to include your own ideas based on information found.

Superstition

I. History of superstitions
   A. Existed in every society throughout history
      1. Many superstitions began in ancient times
      2. Many superstitions are fairly recent
   B. Most people act superstitiously from time to time
   C. Involves many activities
      1. Eating
      2. Working
      3. Sleeping

II. Reasons for superstitions
   A. Fear
   B. Uncertainty about the unknown

III. Kinds of superstitions
   A. Dealing with important events
      1. Birth—a person born on Sunday will have good luck
      2. Marriage—a bride and groom will have bad luck if they see each other on their wedding day
   B. Involving magic—similar actions produce similar results
      1. A newborn baby must be carried upstairs before being carried downstairs so the child will rise in the world and be successful
      2. Put money in a wallet when giving it as a gift to insure that it will always contain money
   C. Involving a deliberate action to cause something to happen
      1. Causing good luck—carrying a rabbit's foot or lucky penny
      2. Avoiding bad luck—not traveling on the 13th of a month

Purpose (thesis)—choose one:

1. Compare superstitions and the use of astrology (horoscopes).
2. Describe the types of superstitions and their origins.
3. Become "superstition" and tell about yourself and your powers.
4. Discuss the reasons for belief in superstitions.
5. Relate how superstitions affect our lives.

Continued next page

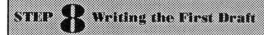

Introduction:

_____

_____

_____

_____

_____

_____

_____

_____

_____

_____

_____

_____

_____

Conclusion:

_____

_____

_____

_____

_____

_____

_____

_____

_____

_____

_____

_____

_____

_____

_____

ON YOUR OWN

Writing the First Draft

You have completed the research for your selected subject and now it's time to examine and write about your findings. If you have taken good notes, this step will be an easy one. The notes, along with your outline, will provide everything you need to write an excellent paper.

Writing a first draft is important because it allows you to focus on the ideas and information you want to include. You can polish and perfect the paper later.

1. Organize the note cards you took for your independent research in Step 6 by arranging them according to the revised outline you wrote in Step 7. To make the task easier, spread the note cards out on a flat surface. Classify the cards first by subtopics and then by details.

2. Once they are in the correct order, number the cards by placing a number in the lower righthand corner.

3. Begin writing your first draft, following the organization of the outline. You may wish to begin with the first main topic and develop it according to the purpose you stated in the thesis, or you may wish to begin with the introduction, which includes your thesis statement.

4. As you write your first draft, keep the following in mind:

   a. Skip two lines between each line to make revisions easier.

   b. If you are uncertain of the spelling of a word or come across a problem, simply put a question mark next to it. This will remind you to check it later, and you will not be interrupting the flow of ideas as you write.

   c. Put the source and page numbers of any statistics or quotations in the margin in order to properly footnote them later.

   d. When necessary, combine ideas from note cards.

   e. Begin the paper with an interesting introduction that will grab the reader's attention. Also, write a conclusion that briefly summarizes the main ideas you've included.

REMINDER: Check off "Step 8: Write the First Draft" on your Student Checklist.

Revising the First Draft

Now that you have completed the first draft, it is time to take a careful look at what you have written. By making the necessary revisions, you will be ready to write your final paper. The following ideas will help you:

1. Use a different color pen when making corrections. This will enable you to easily identify any changes.

2. Check spelling, grammar, punctuation, and sentence and paragraph structure.

3. Check all facts to make sure they are accurate.

4. Use a thesaurus to change any words that are repeated too often or to find a word to substitute for a less-effective one.

5. Make sure that the sentences within each paragraph all deal with the same idea and that the paragraphs follow in a logical order.

6. Make sure that all information included relates to the thesis. Omit information that doesn't fit or reword it in order to make it fit the thesis statement.

7. Check any statistics and quotations to make sure that they are properly indicated and documented.

8. Avoid repetitions, since they tend to make the paper less interesting.

9. Make sure all your points are clear and communicate your ideas to the reader.

10. Do not be afraid to cut what is not needed and to add any information that is missing.

ACTIVITY ONE   *REVISING THE FIRST DRAFT*

Directions: When revising a paper you must look carefully for any mistakes that need correcting. The picture below has 10 mistakes. Circle the mistakes found in the picture.

S T E P

9

REVISING THE FIRST DRAFT ACTIVITY TWO

I. DIRECTIONS: The quotations below have been edited using the editing symbols in the box. On the lines provided, rewrite each quotation correctly.

Editing Symbols

Types of Errors	Examples
Insert punctuation (period, comma, etc.)	St. Paul, Minn. Its late.
New paragraph	for science. ¶ Psychology is
No paragraph	⌐ The next problem
Insert missing words	It is cold outside.
Transpose (change order of words/letters)	Nor they did the following day
Delete (take out words/letters)	can be ~~almost~~ positive
Fix capitalization	Thanksgiving is in November.
Fix spelling error	Don't forget to reherse.
Replace wrong word	I can't here you.

---

1. "France has lost a battle. but france has not lose a war. (De Gaulle)

---

2. "Better starve free then be a fat slave." (Aesop)

---

3. He who fears some thing gives it power overhim." (Moorish proverb)

---

4. "friendship is like money, easier make than kepts. (Samuel Butler)

Continued next page

II. DIRECTIONS: Each of the quotations below has at least one error. Use the editing symbols to indicate the errors you find. Then rewrite the quotation correctly on the lines provided.

1. "Geniuos is one per cent inspiration and ninty- nine cent per perspiration. (Thomas Edison)

_____

2. "Grate hopes make great men." (Thomas Fuller)

_____

3. "Too try may be to dye, but not to care is never to be bourne." (Refield)

_____

4. "To be conscious that you is ignorant are a great step to knwledge." (Disraeli)

_____

III. DIRECTIONS: The paragraph below has many errors. Use the editing symbols or write in the margin to correct the errors you find. Copy the paragraph correctly on the lines provided.

in December 1831 the Choctaw indians were by forced the u.s. government to leave they're home lands in Misisippi and march more then 400 miles to a resarvation near the red river in Texas the indians wore no macasins and only a few clothes and they endured freezing tempratures as they walked threw Little rock Arkansas. Other Indians were treated just as disgracefully? The Seminoles in florida were pushed of their fertil lands threatened and then finaly tricked into migreating to the west. The Creeks rifused to leave their homes and were led out of Alabama in chains

_____

_____

_____

_____

_____

_____

_____

REVISING THE FIRST DRAFT

Directions: On the lines provided below, write a paragraph based on one of the topics listed.
When you have completed your paragraph, give it to an "editing partner." Ask this partner to edit your paragraph, looking for errors in spelling, punctuation, grammar, sentence and paragraph structure, and word choice. Use the editing symbols from Activity 2 when appropriate. Next, give the paragraph to a second editing partner and ask him or her to further edit your paper, using a different colored pen or pencil. Based on the editing done by your two partners, rewrite your paragraph.

> **Topics:**
> I Am the Baseball That Hank Aaron Hit for His 715th Homerun
> The Most Unforgettable Character I Ever Met
> If I Could Go Back in Time, I Would Visit . . .
> My Life as a Piece of Bubblegum

_____

_____

_____

_____

_____

_____

_____

Revised paragraph:

_____

_____

_____

_____

_____

_____

_____

ACTIVITY FOUR   *REVISING THE FIRST DRAFT*

I. DIRECTIONS: When writing a paper, you will want to use the best and most effective words possible. It is also important not to overuse a word. A thesaurus (book of synonyms) can help you locate a variety of words with similar meaning. Using a thesaurus, find four synonyms for each of the words listed.

1. very   _____ _____ _____ _____

2. nice   _____ _____ _____ _____

3. light   _____ _____ _____ _____

4. sad   _____ _____ _____ _____

5. thin   _____ _____ _____ _____

II. DIRECTIONS: Select one of your favorite songs and attach the lyrics to this page. Underline the adjectives and verbs in the song. Rewrite the lyrics, on the lines below, using the synonyms found in the thesaurus for the underlined words.

Lyrics:

_____

_____

_____

_____

_____

_____

Rewritten version:

_____

_____

_____

_____

_____

_____

ON YOUR OWN   Revising the First Draft

Now that you are familiar with editing symbols and the way in which a paper is edited, it is time to edit and revise the first draft you wrote for your independent research paper. Use the checklist below to help you.

Editing Checklist

Title of paper _____   **Editing partner** _____

1. Read your research paper to yourself. Place a check next to each item below when you have satisfactorily completed it.

☐ Check the beginning of your paper. Will the beginning attract and hold the reader's attention?
☐ Check for complete sentences.
☐ Check the organization. Are sentences and paragraphs in the right order?
☐ Check the direct quotations and statistics to be sure they properly give credit to the source.
☐ Check the ending. Does it summarize your research paper in some way?
☐ Have you succeeded in accomplishing your purpose (thesis)?
☐ Have you used a variety of sources?

2. Select a partner and ask him or her to read your paper aloud. Ask your partner the following questions, and listen carefully to the answers. (Take notes if necessary.)

☐ Is the beginning interesting? Are there any suggestions?

☐ Is the paper well organized? Any suggestions?

☐ What do you see as being the main purpose of the paper (its thesis)?

☐ What suggestions can you make to help improve this paper?

3. After the conference with your partner, follow the steps below. Place a check in the box next to each item after you have completed it.

☐ Make changes based on the suggestions your partner made.
☐ Check all spelling (use a dictionary).
☐ Check punctuation.
☐ Use a thesaurus to change any words that are repeated too often or to substitute for a less effective word.

REMINDER: Check off "Step 9: Revise the First Draft" on your Student Checklist.

Writing the Final Copy

You have now completed the revision of your first draft and are ready to begin the last step in the research process. If you have successfully completed the other nine steps, this one will be easy! When writing the final copy, you will need to do the following:

1. Prepare a cover for your research paper. This is called a title page and includes the title of your paper, your name, and the date. The following is one acceptable format you may use:

TITLE OF RESEARCH PAPER

(centered and in capital letters)

Name
Date

2. Prepare your bibliography. This is a listing of all the sources you used for your research and the publishing information for each.

3. Prepare a page for footnotes, depending on your class requirements. Footnotes are notes of explanation or references that give the source of the information in the body of a paper.

NAME   DATE

ACTIVITY ONE   *WRITING THE FINAL COPY*

Preparing a Bibliography

A bibliography is a list of books, magazines, and other sources from which you get information on a certain topic. It is arranged alphabetically, according to the first word, whether it is the author's name, editor's name, name of the book, or title of an article. All the lines in a bibliographic entry except the first one are indented three spaces. There are several accepted formats for writing a bibliography. The examples given below follow one of these formats.

The general format for a book reference is:

> author's name, last name first
> title, underlined
> book edition (if indicated)
> place of publication
> publisher's name in full
> year of publication

Here are some ways to list standard books in a bibliography:

1. No author listed
The Chicago Manual of Style. 13th ed. Chicago: University of Chicago Press, 1982.

2. One author
Lester, James. Writing Research Papers: A Complete Guide. 4th ed. Glenview, Ill.: Scott, Foresman and Company, 1984.

3. Two authors
Corder, Jim W., and Ruszkiewicz, John J. Handbook of Current English. 7th ed. Glenview, Ill.: Scott, Foresman and Company, 1985.

4. Three authors
Berelson, Bernard R.; Lazarsfeld, Paul F.; and McPhee, William. Voting. Chicago: University of Chicago Press, 1954.

5. Edited work
Steward, Joyce S., ed. Contemporary College Reader. 3rd ed. Glenview, Ill.: Scott, Foresman and Company, 1985.

Continued next page

The general format for a periodical (magazine) is:

> author's name, last name first
> title of article, in quotation marks
> name of magazine, underlined
> date of publication
> page reference

Here is how a magazine article is listed:

> Eliot, John L. "Isle Royale." <u>National Geographic</u>, April 1985, pp. 534-550.

Here are ways to list articles in reference works:

1. Author known
<u>The World Book Encyclopedia</u>, 1985 ed. S.v. "Airplane," by Martin Caidin.

2. Author unknown
<u>The World Book Encyclopedia</u>, 1985 ed. S.v. "Antarctic Ocean."

(The abbreviation "S.v." indicates the subject under which you should look.)

Directions: Using the information provided in the box, organize the following into correct bibliographic form.

Book: 1960 Little Women Scholastic Book Services Louisa May Alcott New York

_____

_____

Periodical: Time The Boom Towns June 15, 1987 George J. Church pp. 14-17

_____

_____

Encyclopedia article: ed. 1962 The World Book Encyclopedia Painting

_____

ACTIVITY **TWO**   *WRITING THE FINAL COPY*

Writing Footnotes

Footnotes are notes of explanation or references found at the bottom of the page. Endnotes are references collected at the end of the paper, chapter, or book. Both footnotes and endnotes tell where you can find the source of the information given in the body of the text.

Footnotes and endnotes are indicated in the body of the text by a number that corresponds to the number found in one of the three places where they are recorded. Notes are numbered consecutively (1, 2, 3, . . .). These numbers should be written or typed slightly above the line. They are placed right after the final punctuation marks in the material being quoted or referred to. The first line in a footnote/endnote entry is indented. There are several accepted formats for writing footnotes/endnotes. The examples given below follow one of these formats.

The general format for a footnote/endnote book reference is:

> author's name, as it appears on the title page
> title, underlined
> edition (if indicated)
> place of publication
> publisher's name in full
> year of publication
> page reference

Here are some ways to list books in footnotes:

1. No author listed
The Chicago Manual of Style, 13th ed. (Chicago: University of Chicago Press, 1982), pp. 135-137.

2. One author
James Lester, Writing Research Papers: A Complete Guide, 4th ed. (Glenview, Ill.: Scott, Foresman and Company, 1984), pp. 103-105.

3. Two authors
Jim W. Corder and John J. Ruszkiewicz, Handbook of Current English, 7th ed. (Glenview, Ill.: Scott, Foresman and Company, 1985), p. 50.

4. Three authors
Bernard R. Berelson, Paul F. Lazarsfeld, and William McPhee, Voting (Chicago: University of Chicago Press, 1954), pp. 93-95.

5. Edited work
Joyce S. Steward, Ed., Contemporary College Reader, 3rd ed. (Glenview, Ill.: Scott, Foresman and Company, 1985), pp. 3-5.

Continued next page

The general format for a periodical reference is:

> author's name, as it appears on the title page
> title of article, in quotation marks
> name of magazine, underlined
> date of publication
> page reference

Here is how a magazine article is listed:

> John L. Eliot, "Isle Royale," <u>National Geographic</u>, April 1985, p. 536.

Here are ways to list articles in referenced works:

1. Author known
   <u>The World Book Encyclopedia</u>, 1985 ed. S.v. "Airplane," by Martin Caidin.

2. Author unknown
   <u>The World Book Encyclopedia</u>, 1985 ed. S.v. "Antarctic Ocean."

Often, information regarding the source is included right in the text. This is referred to as "internal footnotes." For example:

> Meinbach and Rothlein (1986) state that traditionally, students have consulted general encyclopedias.

With internal footnotes no notes are necessary at the bottom of the page. The bibliography contains necessary information about the source.

Directions: Using the information provided in the box, organize the following into the correct format for footnotes:

Book: Lancer Books, Inc.   Robert Louis Stevenson   p. 4   New York   1957
                                   Kidnapped

_____

_____

Periodical: 76-89   The Next Frontier?   National Geographic   150.1   Isaac Asimov
                                July 1976

_____

_____

10 Writing the Final Copy

This is it—you have arrived at the last step! You are now ready to write the final copy of your independent research paper.

1. Read through the first draft and make sure that you have made all necessary corrections.

2. Either type the final copy (double spaced) or write legibly in blue or black ink.

3. Prepare a title page to include the title of your research paper (centered in capital letters), and your name and the date (in the lower righthand corner).

4. Center the title of your paper on the first page. This title should be approximately six lines from the top of the page and should be in capital letters.

5. Allow for ample margins on the other three sides of the paper.

6. Prepare your footnote page as you write the final copy. As you come to a statistic, fact, or quotation that you are footnoting, indicate it in the body of the text with a number. Have a sheet of paper headed "Footnotes" and write the corresponding number on this sheet, along with the information required for a footnote. Notes are numbered consecutively (1, 2, 3, . . .). The footnote page should be placed at the end of your paper, just before the bibliography.

7. Prepare your bibliography by placing the index cards with the sources you've used in alphabetical order, by author or by title of source when there is no author (as in the case of encyclopedias). Copy the bibliographic information on a sheet of paper according to the format for writing a bibliography. This should be the last page of your paper.

8. Number all pages in the top righthand corner of the page, except for the title page, footnote page, and bibliography.

9. After you have completed your entire paper, edit it carefully for any final corrections that may need to be made.

10. You should be very proud of yourself. You have done an outstanding job!

REMINDER: Check off "Step 10: Write the Final Copy" on your Student Checklist.

Note: Answers are provided for those activities for which there is only one correct answer. For those activities that are more open ended, evaluation is left to the discretion of the teacher.

Step 2

ACTIVITY 1:
1. Panning for Gold
2. Totem Poles
3. Radiation Therapy
4. Nutrients in Milk

ACTIVITY 2:
1, 2, 4—general
3,5—narrow

Step 3

ACTIVITY 2:
1. 700–799
2. 500–599
3. 800–899
4. 200–299
5. 100–199

1. Music, Mozart, Composers
2. Civil War, Wars, American History
3. Black Holes, Space, Astronomy
4. Baseball, World Series, Sports Events
5. John F. Kennedy, Bay of Pigs, Cuba

ACTIVITY 4:
1. World Almanac
2. World Atlas
3. Familiar Quotations
4. Thesaurus
5. *Current Biography Yearbook*
6. First Facts

Step 5

ACTIVITY 1:
I. Discovering prehistoric man
   A. Archeological digs
   B. Studying fossils
   C. Making models of early man
II. How prehistoric man hunted

I. Choosing and planning for a career
   A. Learning about different careers
   B. Education and training
II. Applying for a job
   A. Writing a resume
   B. Being interviewed

I. History of the airplane
   A. Early experiments and ideas
   B. First manned flights
II. Airplanes in war
   A. Fighter planes
   B. Bombers

ACTIVITY 2:
I. What the moon is like
   A. The moon's surface
      1. Craters
      2. Mountains
      3. Long, narrow valleys
   B. Atmosphere and weather
II. How the moon moves
   A. Orbit
   B. Phases of the moon
      1. New moon
      2. Full moon
      3. Quarter moon

I. What to take
   A. Equipment
   B. Clothing
      1. Comfortable
      2. Washable
   C. Food
      1. Nonperishable
      2. Pure drinking water
II. Making the camp
   A. Location
      1. Near firewood
      2. Near water
   B. Building a campfire
III. Health precautions
   A. Avoid sunburns
   B. Identify poisonous plants

ACTIVITY 3:
1. Hans Christian Andersen's life
2. A. Early childhood
      1. Poor family—one room cottage
      2. Left home at fourteen to seek fortune
   B. Career
      1. Unsuccessful performer, poet, novelist, and playwright
      2. Wrote fairy tales that brought success

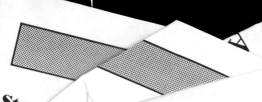

Step

ACTIVITY 1:
1, 6, 8, 12—Fact
2, 3, 4, 7, 9, 10, 11—Opinion

ACTIVITY 2:
1. To provide more food for the fast-growing population.
2. Underwater, in deserts, in space.
3. Sea plants such as kelp and algae.
4. (answers will vary)
5. As a result of the world's increasing population there will be new ways of supplying food. Aquaculture is one way of providing additional food by growing plants underwater.

ACTIVITY 3:
Answers may include:
As it becomes easier to live in space capsules, more civilians who have little or no training will be able to travel in space. The article described the types of crew members who travel on space shuttles.

ACTIVITY 4:
1. Statistic—approximately 2,500,000,000.
2. Fact—increased population, advanced technology.
3. Statistic—1900–1978.
4. Fact—produces dangerous chemical waste.

Step 7

ACTIVITY 1:
I. What myths are about
    A. Mythical beings
    B. Mythical places
    C. Mythical symbols
II. Greek mythology
    A. The creation myth
    B. Greek divinities
    C. Greek heroes
III. Roman mythology
    A. Roman divinity—Jupiter
    B. Roman heroes

I. Early life
II. Early political career
    A. Entry into politics
    B. Youth administrator
III. President, 1963–69
    A. Assassination of President Kennedy
    B. Problems as president
        1. Foreign policy
        2. Vietnam War, etc.

ACTIVITY 3:
I. Clothing
    A. Sleeved undertunic
        1. Wool
        2. Linen
    B. Stockings and leather shoes
    C. Fur-lined long-sleeved coat with hood
II. Armor
    A. Conical helmet
    B. Mail—garment with metal rings
    C. Gauntlets—metal gloves
III. Tournaments
    A. Rules
        1. Governing game
        2. Consequences of breaking rules— imprisonment and loss of property
    B. Events of tournaments
        1. Jousting
        2. Tilting
    C. Weapons
IV. Training to be a knight
    A. Page's training
    B. Squire's training

Step 8

ACTIVITY 1:

	2	
3		5
1		4

Step 9

ACTIVITY 1:
Week misspelled; pears misspelled; 5 upside down on cash register; fishbowl on shelf; child running the cash register; arsenic in the apple juice; peas on the green bean can; numbers on the scale not in order; lady wearing fruit with price on her hat; grocery cart missing one wheel.

ACTIVITY 2:
1. "France has lost a battle. But France has not lost a war."
2. "Better starve free than be a fat slave."
3. "He who fears something gives it power over him."
4. "Friendship is like money, easier made than kept."

ACTIVITY 2 (continued):
1. "Genius is one percent inspiration and ninty-nine percent perspiration."
2. "Great hopes make great men."
3. "To try may be to die, but not to care is never to be born."
4. "To be conscious that you are ignorant is a great step to knowledge."

In December, 1831, the Choctaw Indians were forced by the U.S. government to leave their homelands in Mississippi and march more than 400 miles to a reservation near the Red River in Texas. The Indians wore no moccasins and only a few clothes. They endured freezing temperatures as they walked through Little Rock, Arkansas.

Other Indians were treated just as disgracefully. The Seminoles in Florida were pushed off their fertile lands, threatened, and then finally tricked into migrating to the West. The Creeks refused to leave their homes and were led out of Alabama in chains.

Step 10

ACTIVITY 1:
Alcott, Louisa May. Little Women. New York: Scholastic Book Services, 1960.

Church, George J. "The Boom Towns." Time, June 15, 1987, pp. 14-17.

The World Book Encyclopedia, 1962 ed. S.v. "Painting."

ACTIVITY 2:
Robert Louis Stevenson, Kidnapped (New York: Lancer Books, Inc., 1957), p. 4.

Isaac Asimov, "The Next Frontier?" National Geographic, July 1976, pp. 76-89.